I0789765

THE AGE OF INTELLIGENCE

How AI Will Transform Life in the Coming Decade

By

Gerard McNamara

COPYRIGHT

DISCLAIMER

This book is a work of non-fiction based on the author's research and analysis of current trends in technology. While every effort has been made to ensure the accuracy of the information contained herein, the author and publisher assume no responsibility for errors or omissions. The narrative snapshots of the year 2036 are speculative projections and are intended for illustrative purposes. This book is not intended as a substitute for professional medical, financial, or legal advice.

AI DISCLOSURE

Consistent with the subject matter of this work, artificial intelligence tools were used to assist in the research, editing, and formatting of this manuscript. The author has reviewed, verified, and taken full responsibility for all content.

TO MY WIFE, LUCY

*After the loss of my late wife, Linda, I walked through a long
season of darkness. Grief changes you, and it never disappears. It can
return unexpectedly—through a photograph, a song, or a passing
remark—
and for a moment, you are back there again.*

*Lucy understands this because she carries her own loss.
She loved and lost her husband, Billy. In that shared understanding,
we found something rare: compassion without explanation, love without
conditions, and light without forgetting.*

*Lucy became my light—not by replacing what was lost,
but by standing beside it. Together, we remember Linda and Billy with
gratitude and affection, and we allow joy to exist
alongside remembrance.*

*This book is dedicated to Lucy—for her love, her patience,
and for reminding me that even after profound loss,
life can open its heart once more.*

CONTENTS

Chapter 7
The Intelligent Home 47

Chapter 8
AI Companions: When Loneliness Meets Intelligence 53

Chapter 12
Education Reimagined: Learning That Adapts to You.......................**83**

Chapter 13
Work and Purpose: When Intelligence Transforms Labour..................**89**

Chapter 14
Aging with Dignity: Intelligence That Enables Independence **97**

Chapter 24
What We Must Do: Choices That Will Shape the Next Century 167

Chapter 25
The Future We Choose: Two Paths Ahead 173

Artificial intelligence is often described as a tool: a faster search engine, a clever assistant, a new kind of software.

That description is no longer sufficient.

Across everyday life and across the economy, AI is starting to behave less like an app you choose and more like infrastructure you rely on. It sits underneath decisions and services the way electricity sits underneath modern life: mostly invisible, taken for granted when it works, impossible to ignore when it fails. It recommends, ranks, approves, denies, routes, predicts, flags, and optimises. It decides what you see, what you're offered, what you're charged, and increasingly what you're allowed to do next.

This book is about that shift — and the consequences it brings with it.

When something becomes infrastructure, a predictable pattern follows. Dependence grows. Standards form. Switching becomes painful. Whoever owns and operates the infrastructure gains the power to set the terms: the price of access, the rules of participation, the priority lanes, the exclusions, the appeals process (if any). That is not a moral accusation; it is what infrastructure ownership has always meant.

AI is now entering that category. And that raises a central question: If intelligence becomes essential infrastructure, who gets to own it — and on what terms does the rest of society access it?

We tend to think about AI as a story of capability: smarter systems, faster automation, better predictions, more convenience. Those are real. You will see them throughout this book — in healthcare, education, work, transport, aging, policing, cities, finance, and the everyday tools we use at home.

But capability is only half the story. The other half is power.

AI doesn't only do things. It changes who decides. It changes how decisions are made, how they are justified, and how they can be challenged. It creates new gatekeepers — sometimes human, often automated — and it makes those gatekeepers cheap to scale. It also makes it possible for a handful of organisations to become the default layer through which billions of people and thousands of institutions interact with the world.

That is why this is not only a technology story. It is a governance story.

Over the coming decade, the practical question will not be whether AI spreads. It will. The practical question will be whether we treat it like a private product — owned, controlled, and priced primarily for shareholder return — or whether we insist on the public-interest rules we already apply to other essential systems: transparency, accountability, safety standards, contestability, and meaningful rights to appeal when automated decisions affect people's lives.

This book is written for the intelligent general reader — not as a technical manual, and not as a doom forecast. My aim is simple: to make the shift visible.

Each chapter starts with a concrete situation — a person, a workplace, a service, a decision — and then pulls back to show the wider pattern. If you recognise yourself in these situations, that's the point. AI's biggest impact will not be in headline moments. It will be in the ordinary workings of life: the quiet defaults, the frictionless nudges, the "computer says no" decisions, the systems we adapt to without noticing.

By the end, you'll see why the ownership question matters. Because once infrastructure hardens — once people, firms, and governments build around it — changing it becomes difficult. And if we wait until the dependency is complete, the terms will already have been set.

AI is becoming essential infrastructure. Unless we act soon to govern it in the public interest, intelligence itself will be owned and priced by a few.

This is the age of intelligence. The question is whether we enter it as citizens — or as customers.

Chapter 1

A DAY IN 2036:
LIVING WITH INTELLIGENCE

MORNING: THE CHEN HOUSEHOLD

Sarah Chen's bedroom begins brightening at 6:14 a.m.—sixteen minutes before her alarm is set to ring. The house has learned that she sleeps better when woken gradually, and it has calculated the optimal sunrise simulation based on her sleep patterns over the past three months. By the time the alarm would have sounded, she's already awake, stretching in light that mimics a spring morning even though February rain streaks the windows outside.

"Good morning, Sarah," her home assistant says. "You slept seven hours and twenty-three minutes, with good, deep sleep cycles. Your heart rate variability looks healthy. Maya is still asleep—she has forty minutes before she needs to be up for school."

Sarah is forty-two. She is a single mother and works as an urban planner for the city of Portland. Her daughter, Maya, is twelve, navigating middle school with all the particular challenges that age brings—the social minefields, the shifting friendships, and the homework that somehow takes three times longer than it should. They've lived in this house for three years now, long enough that its intelligent systems have become invisible—part of how life works rather than technology they consciously use.

"The presentation for this morning's meeting is ready for review," her work assistant notes. "I've incorporated the demographic data you requested and created three visualization options. Would you like to see them?"

Sarah scrolls through the visualisations while eating breakfast—oatmeal with berries that the house had delivered yesterday, based on her nutrition goals and current refrigerator inventory. The AI has done solid work on the presentation, organising complex transit data into clear graphics. She makes two adjustments, approves the final version, and sends it to her colleague Neil Bradley, who'll co-present at the meeting.

None of this feels remarkable to her anymore. That is the most noteworthy thing about it.

MAYA'S MORNING

Down the hall, Maya's room begins its own gentle wake-up sequence at 6:50 a.m. Her preferences differ from her mother's—she likes to wake to music rather than a simulated sunrise, and her AI tutor has learned she's more receptive to morning learning if given ten minutes of her favourite songs first. Early adolescent brains work differently, apparently; the research is detailed on this.

"Good morning, Maya," her tutor—whom she's named Aria—says after the music fades. "You have a Spanish quiz today. Would you like to do a quick review while you're getting ready?"

Maya agrees, and Aria begins a conversational vocabulary review while Maya brushes her teeth and chooses clothes. The AI adapts to her distraction, repeating words she misses and celebrating the ones she remembers. It knows she learns better through dialogue than flashcards—something her teachers took years to figure out, but the AI identified within weeks.

"You got seventeen out of twenty," Aria reports as Maya heads to the kitchen. "The three you missed were all in the future tense conjugation. Want me to create a quick game for the bus ride that focuses on those?"

But Sarah sometimes wonders if Maya is learning to work with AI more than with people. Whether that's a problem or the shape of the future, she cannot say.

THE COMMUTE

At 7:35 a.m., Sarah's transportation app alerts her that her vehicle is arriving. She doesn't own a car—hasn't for five years now. Instead, she subscribes to a transportation service that dispatches autonomous vehicles based on her schedule and preferences. It works out cheaper than car ownership once you factor in insurance, maintenance, and parking.

The vehicle that pulls up is configured to her settings: temperature at sixty-eight degrees, news briefing ready to play, and the seat adjusted to her height. Maya's school bus—also autonomous—will arrive in twelve minutes, timed to let Sarah see her off before leaving.

The ride to City Hall takes twenty-two minutes, during which Sarah reviews the news briefing and responds to two emails using voice dictation. The vehicle coordinates with traffic systems throughout the city, timing its speed to hit green lights and merging seamlessly with other autonomous vehicles. Sarah barely notices the driving anymore—it's become background, like an elevator's operation or an escalator's movement.

Her colleague Neil is in another vehicle heading to the same meeting, and their cars coordinate arrival times so they can walk in together—professional courtesy, algorithmically arranged.

"Ready for the council?" he asks through the vehicle's communication system.

"My suggestion included some talking points based on council members' previous questions," Neil Bradley adds. "Surprisingly helpful."

They both still think of AI assistance as "surprising" when it works well—a remnant of an earlier era when such systems were unreliable.

Their children won't share this surprise. For Maya's generation, AI competence is the baseline expectation.

THE WORKPLACE

The city council meeting went well. Sarah presented the transit proposal, fielding questions with help from an earpiece that fed her relevant data in real-time. When a council member asked about comparable programmes in other cities, her AI assistant surfaced case studies she hadn't prepared, giving her concrete examples to cite. The councillor seemed impressed. Sarah silently thanked the algorithm.

After the meeting, she returns to her office to find that her AI has already analysed the council's reactions—identifying which members seemed supportive, which seemed sceptical, and what concerns might need addressing before the vote. It has drafted follow-up emails for her review, personalised messages to each council member addressing their specific questions.

She scans the drafts quickly. Most are good, but one makes her wince—the AI has confused Councillor Reyes with Councillor Martinson, referencing concerns about school funding when Reyes had actually asked about traffic safety. An easy mistake, perhaps, but exactly the kind that could damage a professional relationship. Sarah corrects it, adding a mental note: always review the names. The AI is excellent at patterns but still stumbles on details that matter.

Sarah spends her afternoon on planning work that still requires human judgement: walking a proposed development site, meeting with community members, and weighing competing priorities that resist algorithmic optimisation. The AI handles research, scheduling, documentation, and analysis, freeing her to focus on work that requires presence, intuition, and relationship-building.

She sometimes thinks about her father, who worked as an accountant until he retired fifteen years ago. His job involved work that AI now handles automatically: data entry, reconciliation, and routine analysis. Her career has changed too, but it still exists because urban planning requires understanding communities in ways that AI systems, for all their capabilities, still cannot match. At least not yet. She tries not to think too hard about that "yet."

AFTERNOON: MAYA AT SCHOOL

The history project Maya is working on involves analysing primary sources from the civil rights movement. The AI helps with research—finding documents and transcribing handwritten letters—but the analysis and interpretation are for the students to make. Their teacher has been explicit about this: AI can gather and organise information, but understanding what it means is human work.

Maya finds this distinction frustrating sometimes. Her AI tutor can explain historical events more clearly than her teacher, answer questions instantly, and never get impatient. But she's starting to understand what her teacher means. When her group argues about whether a particular strategy was effective, the AI can provide facts but not a resolution. The judgement is theirs to make. The AI has no stake in the answer.

That matters, she's beginning to realise. Having a stake in things matters.

EVENING: DINNER AND HOMEWORK

Sarah picks up Maya from her orthodontist appointment at 4:30. The orthodontist's office has changed since Sarah wore braces—AI-assisted imaging and treatment plans optimised by machine learning mean fewer appointments and better outcomes.

They stop for Thai food at a restaurant Maya likes. The ordering is AI-assisted—the system knows their preferences—but the experience is human. Mother and daughter share a meal, talking about school, work, and plans for the weekend. The conversation meanders the way good conversations do.

"How's the history project going?" Sarah asks.

"Good. We found some amazing letters. The AI transcribed them, but we had to figure out what they meant. Like, why would someone write something a certain way? What they were trying to say."

"That's the part that matters," Sarah says. "The AI can read the letters. You can understand the people."

At home, Maya finishes homework while Sarah reviews tomorrow's schedule. The house has prepared the living room for their evening routine—lighting adjusted and Maya's favourite throw blanket retrieved from where she'd left it. They watch a film together, something they try to do most evenings. The streaming service recommended it, but Sarah chose it deliberately—an old film she loved as a teenager, wanting to share it with her daughter. The AI can predict what they'll enjoy; it cannot understand why some things matter more than others.

NIGHT: GEORGE SULLIVAN

"Your daughter called while you were at book club," the companion tells him. "She said she'll try again tomorrow evening. Your granddaughter's soccer team won their game."

George smiles at the news. He watches highlights from the game that his companion has queued up—his granddaughter scoring a goal, celebrating with teammates. He cannot attend the matches in person anymore, but the AI ensures he doesn't miss these moments.

He spends the evening reading, with the AI adjusting the lighting to reduce eye strain as it gets darker. When he starts to feel tired, the house notices subtle changes in his posture that signal sleep is approaching.

"It's getting late, George. Would you like me to start your bedtime routine?"

He agrees, and the house begins preparing. Bathroom lights on. Bedroom cooling. Sleep sounds ready to play when he lies down. As he settles into bed, George thinks about Martha. She would have found this technology strange, but she would have been grateful, too—grateful that he can live independently, grateful that loneliness is kept at bay.

"Good night, George," the companion says. "Sleep well."

THE DAY ENDS

Back in the Chen household, Sarah checks on Maya—asleep with her tablet still glowing beside her. She removes it, adjusts the covers, and watches her daughter breathe for a moment. The house notices and dims the hallway lights as she moves towards her own room.

"Tomorrow's schedule is confirmed," her assistant says quietly. "Your 9 a.m. meeting was moved to 9:30. Maya has a study group after school."

Twenty years ago, Sarah would have found this day remarkable. Now it is ordinary. A Tuesday in 2036, shaped by intelligence woven so thoroughly into daily life that its absence would be more noticeable than its presence. The technology doesn't make her life perfect. She still worries about Maya's social development. She still misses human connections that technology cannot provide. But the technology handles complexity so she can focus on what matters. It remembers, so she doesn't have to. It coordinates so she can live.

As she falls asleep, her house continues to watch—monitoring security, adjusting the climate, and preparing for tomorrow. The intelligence that surrounds her never sleeps. Whether that's wonderful or unsettling probably depends on your perspective. For Sarah, tonight, it is true.

This is ordinary life in 2036. Not perfect. Not transformed beyond recognition. Just life, with intelligence woven in, doing what technology has always done: extending human capability, one day at a time.

Chapter 2

FIRE:
THE FIRST TECHNOLOGY REVOLUTION

A LIGHT IN THE DARKNESS

Picture a night one million years ago in what is now South Africa. A small band of early humans—our distant ancestors, though they'd scarcely recognise us—huddles near the entrance of Wonderwerk Cave.

The darkness presses in from all sides: thick, almost suffocating.

Beyond the cave mouth, predators are on the prowl. Leopards. Hyenas.

Creatures with teeth and claws against which human bodies offer precious little defense.

For hundreds of thousands of years, this was how things were. Darkness meant danger. Night meant vulnerability. Sleep meant risk. You closed your eyes and hoped you'd open them again come morning.

Then someone—we'll never know who, and isn't that strange to think about?—carried a burning branch into that cave.

Perhaps lightning had struck a tree nearby. Maybe a brush fire had swept through the valley, leaving smouldering embers that an inquisitive individual decided to preserve rather than flee from. However it happened, that flickering flame changed absolutely everything. The shadows retreated. The predators kept their distance. And for the first time, humans could rest through the night without the constant vigilance that exhaustion had always demanded.

Archaeologists have found evidence of controlled fire use at Wonderwerk Cave dating back roughly one million years—ash layers, burned bone fragments, and charred plant remains that accumulated not from wildfires sweeping through the cave, but from fires deliberately maintained within the cave's shelter. These early humans weren't merely encountering fire; they were keeping it and tending it. They had begun to transform a force of nature into a tool of survival.

Fire was humanity's first technology. Full stop. And the pattern of how we adopted it—initial fear, gradual understanding, eventual dependence, and finally transformation—would repeat with every major technology that followed, including the one reshaping our world today.

FROM TERROR TO TOOL

Long before civilization, long before farming or writing or cities, fire existed as something dazzling, dangerous, and seemingly alive. Lightning strikes could burn entire forests in hours. Volcanic eruptions produced flames hot enough to melt rock. Early humans viewed fire as a power belonging to the gods—something of the sky, the earth, nature itself.

Not something for people to mess about with.

But curiosity—our oldest survival tool, when you think about it—pushed humans closer to understanding this mysterious force. The journey from fearing fire to controlling it took hundreds of thousands of years. Not exactly a quick study, were we?

First came opportunistic use: taking advantage of natural fires to scavenge cooked meat from burned carcasses, which provided more calories and fewer parasites than raw flesh. A bit grim, perhaps, but effective.

Then came fire maintenance—keeping flames alive through careful tending, carrying embers from camp to camp, and protecting the precious heat source from rain and wind like your life depended on it. Because it did.

The final breakthrough—creating fire at will through friction, sparks, or flint—may not have been thoroughly mastered until 400,000 years ago. This transformation from fire-keeper to fire-maker marked one of humanity's most incredible cognitive leaps. We'd learned not merely to use what nature provided, but to generate it ourselves, on demand, wherever we needed it.

Fire had become the first technology entirely under human control. And nothing would ever be quite the same.

WHAT FIRE MADE POSSIBLE

The effects of controlled fire cascaded through every aspect of human existence. Warmth during freezing nights allowed human populations to spread beyond tropical Africa into colder climates—places our hairless, thin-skinned bodies had no business being, frankly. Protection from predators enabled longer, deeper sleep. Neuroscientists now understand that quality sleep is essential for memory consolidation and cognitive development. Some researchers argue— and I find this rather marvellous—that fire literally made us smarter by giving our brains the rest they needed to grow.

Cooking transformed nutrition in ways we are still coming to appreciate.

Raw meat requires a great deal of chewing and yields limited caloric intake. Cooked food delivers more energy for less digestive work, while killing parasites and neutralising toxins that would otherwise cause illness. Over generations, human jaws and teeth shrank—we no longer needed the massive chewing apparatus of our ancestors—while our brains grew larger, fuelled by the surplus calories that cooking provided.

Fire extended the day itself. In a world without artificial light, darkness meant the end of productive activity. Fire pushed back that boundary, creating hours for toolmaking, for planning, and for teaching the young. Light became something humans controlled rather than something imposed by the planet's rotation. Think about that for a moment: we'd started bending time itself to our purposes.

Fire-hardened wooden spears made hunting more effective. Fire cleared land for travel and settlement. It created charcoal, an early fuel that would later enable metallurgy. Each capability built upon the last, compounding across generations into advantages no other species could hope to match.

THE FIRST SOCIAL NETWORK

Perhaps fire's most profound impact was social. And I don't use that word lightly.

The campfire became humanity's original gathering place—a shared warmth drawing people together, a light defining the boundary between the safety of the group and the danger of the wild beyond. Around those flames, something new emerged: Community. Culture. Us.

Anthropologists studying modern hunter-gatherer societies have observed something fascinating: daytime conversation focuses primarily on practical matters—where to find food, how to make tools, who did what to whom. But nighttime conversation around fires? That shifts dramatically towards storytelling, singing, discussion of social relationships, and the sharing of knowledge with no immediate practical application. The campfire created space for culture itself.

Language likely evolved alongside fire use. The shared experience of sitting together through long evenings created both the opportunity and the need for more complex communication. Stories could be told. Plans could be explained. Knowledge accumulated across generations through oral traditions that the campfire made possible.

Fire didn't just keep us warm; it made us human in ways extending far beyond biology. The campfire was, in a very real sense, humanity's first social network. It was a technology that connected minds, enables the sharing of information, and creates communities bound by something more than genetic kinship.

The pattern would repeat with every communication technology that followed: writing, printing, the telegraph, the telephone, and the internet. Each created new ways for humans to gather, share, and build upon collective knowledge. The campfire was simply the first.

THE PATTERN OF REVOLUTION

Fire established a pattern that would repeat with every transformative technology in human history. It is worth laying out explicitly, because we'll see it again and again throughout this book.

First comes discovery—the recognition that something powerful exists, even if we don't fully understand it. Then comes fear—awareness of the dangers and the destruction this force can cause when uncontrolled.

Gradually, through experimentation and accumulated knowledge, comes mastery—the ability to harness the technology reliably for human purposes.

With mastery comes dependence. Once humans controlled fire, they could no longer survive without it. Populations expanded into regions that required fire for warmth. Diets had adapted to cooked food. Social structures had formed around the campfire's gathering power. There was no going back to a world before fire—the technology had become essential to human existence. The door had closed behind us.

Finally comes transformation. Fire didn't just solve problems existing before its mastery; it created entirely new possibilities that previous generations couldn't have imagined. Metallurgy, ceramics, and the chemical transformations that eventually led to modern industry—none of these were the goals driving the initial adoption of fire. They emerged from capabilities fire created, possibilities becoming visible only once the technology was thoroughly integrated into human life.

This pattern—discovery, fear, mastery, dependence, transformation—will appear throughout this book. The wheel, metal tools, the steam engine, electricity, computers: each followed the same arc, and each ultimately changed humanity in ways its early adopters never anticipated.

THE FIRE OF OUR TIME

Artificial intelligence is humanity's new fire. I realise that sounds grandiose, but bear with me.

Like fire, it appears both wondrous and terrifying. Like fire, it promises to extend human capability beyond biological limits. Like fire, it will create dependencies we can barely imagine and transformations we cannot yet predict.

Fire extended our physical reach—we could shape materials, inhabit territories, and survive conditions our bodies alone could never handle.

AI extends our cognitive reach—we can process information, recognise patterns, and solve problems at scales our minds alone cannot manage.

The parallel runs deeper than you might initially suppose.

We are somewhere in the middle of the pattern now. Discovery has happened—AI capabilities that seemed impossible a decade ago are now routine, almost dull. Fear is widespread, and not without reason—the technology carries genuine risks, which this book will examine honestly.

Mastery remains incomplete—we're still learning what AI can do, how to direct it, and how to prevent its misuse.

Dependence is already emerging. Systems we rely upon daily—from search engines to navigation to medical diagnosis—increasingly incorporate AI in ways most users never see or think about. And transformation is underway, though we cannot yet perceive its full scope, any more than our ancestors around that first campfire could have imagined cities, civilization, or the world their descendants would build.

Every breakthrough following fire—tools, farming, cities, machinery—traces its lineage back to that first controlled flame.

Every breakthrough following AI will trace its lineage back to this moment. We are living through a transition as significant as the one occurring in Wonderwerk Cave a million years ago.

Fire was humanity's first step towards shaping its own future. AI may be the step that determines what that future ultimately becomes.

Chapter 3

THE WHEEL:
THE FIRST REVOLUTION IN MOVEMENT

A REVOLUTION IN THE DUST

Sometime around 3500 BCE, in the river-fed plains of Mesopotamia, a potter sat at his workspace shaping clay. His hands guided the material on a rotating stone disc—a device that made it far easier to form symmetrical vessels than working freehand. Potters had used such wheels for generations, spinning clay into bowls and jars with an efficiency that hand-building could never hope to match.

But on this day—or one very like it, in circumstances we can only imagine—someone looked at that spinning disc and saw something beyond pottery.

Perhaps it was the potter himself, struck by a sudden flash of insight.

Maybe a merchant watching nearby, frustrated beyond measure by the limits of what donkeys could carry on their backs. Perhaps a builder struggling to shift stone blocks, requiring dozens of workers to drag them even short distances. Whoever it was, they grasped a principle that would reshape civilization: a circle rotating on an axis could do more than shape clay.

It could move the world.

The insight seems blindingly obvious now. But here's the thing—for hundreds of thousands of years, humans had walked this earth without conceiving it. No animal had evolved wheels. No natural process suggested the solution. The wheel required imagining something that didn't exist in nature—a shape serving a purpose nature had never demonstrated. It was pure human abstraction made physical. And it changed absolutely everything.

THE SIMPLE INVENTION THAT CHANGED EVERYTHING

The wheel is one of humanity's simplest inventions: a circular object rotating around an axle. No moving parts besides that rotation. No complex mechanisms. Just a shape and a principle—reducing friction by rolling instead of dragging.

Yet this simple invention transformed human civilization more profoundly than almost any technology that followed. Before the wheel, humans moved only what they could carry. After the wheel, they moved entire civilisations.

Within centuries of its invention, wheeled carts spread across the ancient world, revolutionising trade, warfare, agriculture, and daily life in ways nobody could have anticipated. Cities grew larger because food could be transported from greater distances. Armies became mobile forces capable of conquering distant territories. Knowledge spread as traders carried ideas along with goods—sometimes the ideas proved more valuable than the merchandise.

For hundreds of thousands of years, humans had travelled at the speed of walking. Roughly three miles per hour, if you were making decent progress. The wheel didn't directly change human speed, but it changed what humans could carry. A person can carry perhaps fifty pounds for any real distance before collapsing from exhaustion. A wheeled cart pulled by an animal can shift thousands of pounds without breaking a sweat.

(Well, the animal sweats. You take my point.) This increase in carrying capacity reshaped how humans lived. It sounds dry when put that way, but think about what it actually meant: everything changed.

THE TRUE GENIUS: THE AXLE

The wheel gets all the credit, but honestly? The axle was the true breakthrough. A wheel without a proper axle is merely a rolling log—useful enough for shifting stones short distances, but utterly incapable of supporting a vehicle.

The engineering challenge wasn't creating a circular shape. Any fool can make a circle. The challenge was to create a system in which that shape could rotate freely while bearing weight, maintaining alignment, and resisting forces that would tear a crude assembly apart. Early wheelwrights faced problems demanding precise solutions.

The axle had to be smooth enough to allow rotation but tight enough to prevent wobbling. The holes in the wheel had to match the axle's diameter exactly—too loose and the wheel falls off mid-journey; too tight and friction prevents it from turning at all. The wood had to be strong enough to bear loads without splitting, yet workable enough to shape with primitive tools. Getting all this right simultaneously was fiendishly difficult.

These challenges explain why the wheel appeared relatively late in human development—thousands of years after we'd mastered fire, tools, and even agriculture. The concept was simple. The execution required accumulated knowledge of materials, precise craftsmanship, and the sort of iterative problem-solving that produces reliable technology. The wheel's apparent simplicity conceals the sophistication needed to make the blessed thing actually work.

THE FAMILIAR ARC

The wheel followed the same arc fire had traced—though with its own character.

The initial insight came when someone saw rotational motion as transportation rather than pottery-making. Early wheeled vehicles were dangerous and unpredictable, prone to collapse, difficult to control on slopes, and entirely capable of crushing those unfortunate enough to fall beneath them. But fear was less acute than with fire—wheels don't burn down your village, after all.

Mastery accumulated over generations as wheelwrights refined their craft. They developed spoked wheels that were lighter and stronger, bearings that reduced friction, and designs suited to different terrains and purposes. The knowledge passed from master to apprentice, improving incrementally across centuries.

Dependence emerged as societies restructured around wheeled transportation. Cities along trade routes couldn't survive without the wheels of commerce. Armies relying on supply wagons couldn't campaign without them. Farmers who could transport surplus to distant markets couldn't return to subsistence agriculture even if they'd wanted to. The wheel became an essential infrastructure for civilization. There was no going back.

Transformation followed as the wheel enabled possibilities its inventors never imagined. Gears—wheels with teeth transferring rotational force—made complex machinery possible. Pulleys—wheels redirecting tension—enabled construction on scales that muscle alone could never achieve. Water wheels and windmills—wheels turned by natural forces—provided power that would drive early industry.

The simple principle of rolling instead of dragging has cascaded into technologies that reshape what human societies can build and accomplish.

THE MULTIPLICATION OF EFFORT

The wheel didn't make humans faster or stronger. What it did was make human effort more effective—the same energy could accomplish far more when applied through wheels than through carrying. A farmer could harvest ten times more grain with a wheeled cart than by lugging loads on his back. This surplus enabled specialisation. Some people could focus on crafts or governance instead of everyone farming for bare subsistence.

Cities formed where surplus food could be transported and stored. Armies equipped with wheeled chariots dominated those without; the chariot transformed warfare from close-quarters combat between foot soldiers to mobile forces that struck quickly and retreated faster. Empires rose and fell based partly on who mastered wheeled warfare most effectively.

Trade expanded exponentially. Merchants could transport goods across hundreds of miles, connecting distant civilisations in ways previously unimaginable. Silk travelled from China to Rome. Spices from India reached Europe. Ideas, technologies, and cultures mixed in ways that were impossible when humans could carry only what they personally needed.

Consider Ahmose, a merchant in ancient Egypt around 1500 BCE. His father had traded pottery along the Nile, carrying what he could on his back, serving villages within a day's walk. Ahmose inherited the trade but not its limitations. With a donkey cart, he could carry twenty times what his father managed and travel ten times as far. Within a decade, he'd established trading routes spanning hundreds of miles, his network of suppliers and customers dwarfing anything his father could have imagined. He grew wealthy. His children learned to read. His grandchildren would become scribes and officials. But Ahmose's success meant others' failure. The village traders who couldn't afford carts watched their customers vanish. The porter who once carried goods for merchants found himself replaced by wheels. Progress rarely distributes its gifts evenly—a truth as old as the wheel itself.

THE INEQUALITY OF INNOVATION

The wheel's history reveals a pattern recurring with every transformative technology: not everyone benefits equally, and the gains often flow to those already advantaged. This isn't comfortable to acknowledge, but it's essential.

Civilisations adopting the wheel conquered those that didn't. The chariot armies of Bronze Age empires swept across peoples still fighting on foot. This wasn't because wheeled societies were morally superior or their people inherently more capable. They had a tool multiplying military effectiveness, and that multiplication decided the fate of nations. Brutal, but true.

Within societies, merchants with carts accumulated wealth faster than those carrying goods on their backs. Farmers with wheeled equipment outproduced those working by hand. The technology created winners and losers not because it was designed to do so, but because any tool multiplying capability amplifies existing advantages. Those who could afford wheels gained more than those who couldn't. The gap widened with each generation.

Geographic inequality emerged as well. Some terrains were suited to wheels; others weren't. The flat plains of Mesopotamia and the steppes of Central Asia became highways for wheeled commerce. Mountainous regions, dense forests, and sandy deserts remained barriers that wheels couldn't easily cross. Infrastructure shaped destiny—and building it required resources that not all people possessed in equal measure.

This pattern—technology amplifying inequality even as it increases total capability—will appear throughout this book. It is not unique to the wheel or to AI. It is inherent in how powerful tools interact with existing social structures. Understanding this pattern is essential to thinking clearly about how artificial intelligence might affect our own societies.

EXTENDING REACH, EXTENDING MIND

Like the wheel, AI doesn't make humans fundamentally different. It extends what human intelligence can accomplish.

A human analyst can perhaps process a few dozen research papers, identify patterns, and produce solid work, but is limited by the hours in a day and the capacity of a single mind. An AI system can process millions of papers, identify patterns that no human would notice, and suggest connections that advance entire fields of research. The human intelligence hasn't changed—but its reach has expanded beyond recognition.

A doctor can recall the symptoms and treatments for hundreds of conditions, drawing on years of training and experience. Impressive, certainly. An AI diagnostic system has instant access to every medical journal ever published, every case study, and every treatment outcome.

The doctor's judgement remains essential—perhaps more critical than ever—but the information available to that judgement expands exponentially.

The wheel let humans move more. AI lets humans think more—not in the sense of becoming smarter, but in the sense of applying intelligence across scales and complexities exceeding unaided human capacity. The principle is identical: a tool that reduces friction, multiplies capability, and transforms what individuals and societies can accomplish.

THE PRINCIPLE BEHIND THE WHEEL

The wheel works because it converts sliding friction into rolling friction. Dragging something across the ground requires enormous force because every point of contact resists movement. Rolling something on wheels means only a minor point touches the ground at any given moment, dramatically reducing friction. Simple physics, really. But the implications weren't simple at all.

This principle—reducing friction to make movement easier—applies beyond physical transportation. AI reduces friction in information processing, decision-making, and problem-solving. Tasks requiring hours of human effort—searching through databases, translating languages, analysing medical images—become nearly instantaneous. The friction of information work drops dramatically, just as the wheel dropped the friction of physical work.

But reducing friction has consequences worth pondering. When movement becomes easy, people move more. When information processing becomes easy, people process more information. The efficiency doesn't necessarily mean people work less—it often means they accomplish more in the same time, or that standards for what's considered adequate work rise to match new capabilities. The goalposts shift.

THE WHEEL IN 2036

By 2036, transportation will have evolved far beyond simple wheels, yet the principle remains fundamental. Autonomous vehicles still use wheels.

High-speed trains use wheels. Even spacecraft use wheeled landing gear.

The 5,500-year-old invention persists because the physics haven't changed—rolling remains more efficient than any alternative for surface transportation.

What has changed is the intelligence controlling the wheels. Vehicles navigate themselves. Traffic coordinates automatically. Transportation systems optimise in real-time. The wheel moves us. AI decides where, when, and how.

This layering of technologies—ancient principles enhanced by modern intelligence—characterises much of how AI transforms the world. We don't abandon what works. We add intelligence to make it work better.

The wheel taught humanity that tools extending our physical capabilities reshape civilization. AI is teaching us that tools extending our cognitive capabilities will reshape civilization even more profoundly.

The wheel didn't just transport goods—it transported human civilization itself into a new era. AI is doing the same for human intelligence, carrying us into an age where the friction of thinking, analysing, and deciding drops as dramatically as the wheel once dropped the friction of moving, building, and trading.

We're still in the earliest days of this transformation, roughly equivalent to the first centuries after the wheel's invention, when civilisations were beginning to grasp what this simple tool would make possible over millennia. The journey has barely begun.

Chapter 4

METAL AND TOOLS:
SHAPING CIVILIZATION

THE MOMENT ROCK BECAME SOMETHING ELSE

Sometime around 5000 BCE, in the highlands of what is now Turkey, a man tending a fire noticed something decidedly strange. The rocks ringing his hearth—greenish stones he'd gathered without much thought—were weeping. Bright droplets oozed from their surfaces, pooling in the ash, glowing with the fire's heat.

When the flames died and the droplets cooled, they had hardened into something that wasn't rock at all. Something that gleamed. Something that bent when struck instead of shattering.

He had discovered copper, though he had no name for it. What he understood was more straightforward and more profound: fire could transform rock into something entirely new. The solid Earth itself could be remade. Think about that for a moment: rock becoming... not rock. It must have seemed like pure magic.

This accidental discovery—repeated independently across the ancient world wherever copper-bearing rocks met sufficiently hot flames—launched humanity into an entirely new relationship with the physical world. For hundreds of thousands of years, humans had worked with materials as nature provided them: stone, bone, wood, and fibre.

Now they could create materials that didn't exist until human action brought them into being.

The age of making had begun.

FIRE'S GREATEST GIFT

Metallurgy was impossible without fire. The discovery described in Chapter 2—humanity's first significant technological breakthrough—was the essential prerequisite for this second one. Fire provided warmth, protection, cooked food, and extended the day. But fire's greatest gift may well have been metal. Copper melts at about 1,085 degrees Celsius. Bronze requires similar temperatures. Iron demands even more—nearly 1,540 degrees. These temperatures occur in nature only during volcanic eruptions and lightning strikes. Only sustained, controlled fire, concentrated and intensified through bellows and furnace design, could reliably transform ore into metal.

The mastery of fire, which our ancestors achieved around campfires, eventually enabled the forges that built civilisations. This is how progress works: each breakthrough lays the foundation for the next. Fire enabled metal. Metal enabled complex tools. Complex tools enabled agriculture, construction, and, eventually, the machines that powered the Industrial Revolution.

Technologies don't exist in isolation; they build upon one another in chains of capability spanning millennia. Pull one link and the whole thing unravels.

THE DISCOVERY THAT CHANGED EVERYTHING

Early humans used stone for hundreds of thousands of years—sharp flakes for cutting, heavy rocks for crushing, carefully shaped hand axes for butchering. Stone tools were adequate but limited. Stone is brittle; it breaks unpredictably. It can be sharpened but not shaped into complex forms. It serves, but it constrains.

Metal changed everything. Around 3000 BCE, humans discovered that certain rocks, when heated to extreme temperatures, melted into a liquid that could be poured into moulds and would harden into shapes stone could never achieve. This molten rock, when cooled, became metal—stronger than stone, more durable, and infinitely shapeable.

Bronze was the first alloy, a mixture of copper and tin. Then came iron, more complex and more abundant. Then steel, combining iron with carbon to create a material stronger than anything nature provided. Each advance in metallurgy enabled new tools, new structures, and new possibilities.

Metal tools cut deeper, lasted longer, and could be repaired rather than replaced. Metal weapons transformed warfare. Metal ploughs revolutionised agriculture. Metal nails and bolts enabled complex construction. Every advance in what humans could build or create depended on advances in metalworking.

The Bronze Age, the Iron Age, the Steel Age—we name entire eras of human history after the metals defining what was possible. Metal wasn't just a material; it was the skeleton of civilization, the foundation on which everything else was built.

THE FAMILIAR ARC

Metal traced the same trajectory as fire and the wheel—but with unique intensity. When ancient peoples first observed copper flowing from heated rock, it must have seemed like alchemy made real. Metallurgy was dangerous work: toxic fumes, molten materials, temperatures that could kill instantly. Smelters and smiths were often regarded with superstition, practitioners of an art seeming to border on sorcery.

The knowledge accumulated over generations—which ores yielded which metals, how to control temperature, when to quench and when to anneal.

This expertise was guarded jealously, passed from master to apprentice, giving its possessors economic and military advantages they had no intention of sharing.

Eventually, societies restructured around metal completely. Armies equipped with bronze couldn't face iron-armed opponents. Farmers with metal ploughs couldn't return to wooden ones—their populations had grown beyond what primitive agriculture could support. The technology had become civilization's skeleton.

THE KEEPERS OF SECRETS

In a village in ancient Anatolia, a master smith named his apprentice after seven years of training. The young man had spent those years learning secrets that would never be written down: how to read the colour of heated metal, when the moment was right to strike, and which prayers to offer at each stage of the forging. The knowledge existed only in the hands, eyes, and memories of those who practiced the craft.

This pattern—specialised knowledge transmitted through direct apprenticeship, guarded as a competitive advantage—characterised metallurgy for millennia. The Hittites dominated the ancient Near East partly because they mastered iron smelting while their neighbours still worked bronze. They guarded their techniques as state secrets, understanding that knowledge itself was power.

The parallel to artificial intelligence is striking. AI development today is concentrated among those with specialised knowledge—machine learning engineers, data scientists, and researchers at major technology companies and universities. This expertise took years to develop and isn't easily transferred. The organisations mastering AI gain advantages they're reluctant to share.

Knowledge concentration creates power concentration, as it did when a privileged few held the secrets of metallurgy. Some things don't change much across five thousand years.

RESHAPING THE PHYSICAL WORLD

Metal did more than provide better tools; it fundamentally changed the relationship between humans and the physical world.

Stone tools limited what humans could cut, shape, or build to materials softer than stone itself. Metal tools could cut stone. This opened landscapes for quarrying, construction, and monument-building, defining ancient civilisations. The pyramids, temples, and fortifications still standing thousands of years later were possible because metal tools could shape stone. We often forget this when marvelling at ancient wonders—someone had to carve those massive blocks, and they didn't do it with their fingernails.

Metal changed agriculture from subsistence farming to surplus production. Iron ploughs could break soil too hard for wooden ploughs.

Metal sickles and scythes facilitated faster harvesting. Metal tools for irrigation and water management enabled farming in regions that couldn't support crops with primitive implements. The surplus food from metal-enabled agriculture freed people to specialise in crafts, governance, art, and innovation.

Warfare was transformed completely. Bronze weapons defeated stone weapons. Iron weapons defeated bronze. Steel armour could withstand blows that would shatter earlier protection. The civilisations mastering metallurgy conquered those that hadn't. Empires rose and fell based partly on who had better metal and knew how to work it most effectively.

Grim, but historically accurate.

But metal's most profound impact was on what humans could build. Bridges could span distances impossible with wood or stone alone. Buildings could be constructed taller with metal reinforcement. Machines with metal gears and shafts could mechanically amplify human effort. Metal didn't just make existing tasks easier—it made entirely new categories of construction possible.

METAL IS THE SKELETON OF MODERN CIVILIZATION

Look around any modern city. Metal is everywhere, usually hidden but essential.

The building you're in stands because of metal reinforcement in its concrete. The bridge you crossed today relies on steel cables or beams.

The car, train, or plane that transported you is built around a metal frame. The electrical grid powering your life is composed of metal wires. The water and gas reaching your home flow through metal pipes.

Remove metal from modern civilization, and it collapses. Not gradually—instantly. Buildings fall. Transportation stops.

Communication networks fail. Manufacturing halts. Agriculture becomes impossible at scale.

This isn't obvious because metal is often invisible—buried in concrete, hidden in walls, underground in pipes and cables. But metal is the skeleton holding modern life together, just as actual skeletons hold bodies together. Everything else depends on this hidden structure.

This dependence on invisible, essential infrastructure parallels humanity's emerging reliance on AI. Data centres, fibre optic networks, computational infrastructure—these are becoming the skeleton of modern civilization, just as metal has been for centuries. Most people never see this infrastructure. But remove it, and contemporary life collapses as completely as it would without metal.

FROM FORGE TO ALGORITHM

Metal extended what humans could do with physical force. AI extends what humans can do with cognitive effort. The parallel is really quite precise.

A blacksmith with metal tools can shape materials that a craftsperson with stone tools never could. An engineer with AI design tools can optimise structures that a human working alone couldn't calculate in a lifetime. Both extend human capability by providing tools that amplify effort.

Metal enabled the construction of medieval cathedrals—structures so complex they took generations to build, requiring engineering knowledge accumulated and refined across decades. AI enables the construction of equally complex systems—power grids that balance supply and demand across continents, supply chains that coordinate millions of components, and financial networks that process trillions of transactions.

The parallel runs deeper still. Just as metalworking required specialised knowledge—how to heat ore to the appropriate temperature, which alloys produce which properties, and how to forge without brittleness—AI requires specialised knowledge that most people don't have. Both technologies concentrate power among those who master them.

Both create economic advantages that compound over time. And both, once established as essential infrastructure, become nearly impossible to give up.

A civilization adopting metal tools cannot return to stone—the population it supports, the structures it builds, and the complexity it enables all depend on metal. Similarly, a civilization adopting AI infrastructure cannot readily revert to human-only decision-making. The scale and complexity enabled by AI become essential to maintaining modern life. The door closes behind us, as it always does.

LESSONS FROM THE FORGE

The history of metalworking offers lessons for the AI age—if we're willing to learn them.

Metallurgy didn't spread evenly. Some civilisations developed bronze, while others still used stone. Some mastered iron while others struggled with bronze. These gaps in capability translated directly into military, economic, and political power. The civilisations with superior metal technology conquered those without it.

AI is following the same pattern. Some nations invest heavily in AI research and development. Others lag decades behind. Some companies master AI tools and dominate their industries. Others fail to adapt and disappear. The technology gap creates a power gap that widens over time unless deliberate efforts narrow it.

Metalworking also had environmental consequences that took centuries to recognise. Mining scarred landscapes. Smelting polluted air and water.

Deforestation for charcoal fuel changed regional climates. The benefits were immediate and obvious. The costs were distributed, delayed, and easy to ignore until they became severe.

AI similarly creates consequences we're only beginning to recognise—energy consumption by data centres, the environmental impact of manufacturing computer hardware, and resource extraction for rare-earth elements. The benefits appear immediately; the costs accumulate invisibly.

Perhaps most importantly, metalworking taught humanity that tools extending capability also concentrate power. The blacksmith who could forge superior weapons had influence. The nation with better steel production had a military advantage. The company with advanced manufacturing had economic dominance. Tools aren't neutral—they amplify existing inequalities while creating new ones.

LOOKING FORWARD

By 2036, AI infrastructure will be as essential and as invisible as metal infrastructure is today. Buildings will contain AI-designed components optimised beyond what human engineers could calculate.

Transportation systems will operate on AI-optimised routes, with AI-managed traffic. Manufacturing will happen in factories where AI systems coordinate supply chains spanning continents.

Most people will never see this infrastructure, just as most people never see the metal beams holding up their buildings. But it will be there, fundamental and essential, enabling a civilization more complex than previous generations could have imagined.

Metal is the skeleton of modern civilization. AI is becoming its nervous system—coordinating, optimising, and responding to conditions faster than human management ever could.

The metal age taught humanity what's possible when tools extend physical capability. The AI age is teaching us what's possible when tools extend cognitive capability. Both transformations are irreversible. Both create new dependencies. Both concentrate power while also extending capability to those who gain access.

Metal didn't just change what humans could build. It changed what civilization could be. AI is doing the same—not replacing human intelligence, but extending it to scales and levels of complexity, reshaping what human society can accomplish.

We're building on foundations laid by metal. We're adding intelligence to infrastructure. The combination will define the next century of human development as profoundly as metal defined the previous five millennia.

Chapter 5

THE POWER REVOLUTIONS: STEAM AND ELECTRICITY

For millennia, human progress was limited by the power of muscle—human and animal. Fire, the wheel, and metal had transformed civilization, but they couldn't overcome the fundamental constraint of physical strength.

Then came two revolutionary technologies that would shatter this limitation forever. First, the steam engine harnessed the power of heat and pressure to drive machines with unprecedented force. Then electricity—invisible, instantaneous, and infinitely versatile—would power everything from factories to homes. Together, these power revolutions changed the fabric of modern life.

Samuel Mitchell's hands moved across the loom with the practiced rhythm of twenty years. In his workshop in Manchester, 1825, he could weave eight yards of cotton cloth in a good week—enough to feed his family and maintain the modest dignity of skilled work.

Then the mill opened down the road.

The sound reached him first: a deep mechanical breathing that never stopped, day or night. Steam engines driving power looms, forty of them in endless rows. Samuel walked past one morning and watched through the tall windows, mesmerised and horrified in equal measure.

The machines produced in one hour what took him a week. The cloth wasn't as fine as his, but it was one-tenth the price. Quality couldn't compete with quantity.

Within a year, his orders dried up completely. The machine that destroyed his livelihood also made his children's clothes affordable.

His daughter had three dresses now instead of one.

Progress, they called it. Progress felt like drowning in the tide.

A WORLD HELD BACK BY MUSCLE

Progress was slow, constrained by fundamental natural factors. A city could grow only as large as its surrounding farmland could feed it.

Human civilization was bound by the rhythms of the seasons and the limits of living muscle.

But by the 1700s, England's growing economy demanded more coal. Mines dug deeper to meet the demand, and the deeper they went, the more they flooded. Some mines employed hundreds of men to lift water. England was running out of its most critical resource, not because the coal wasn't there, but because it was drowning.

The crisis demanded a solution. Human muscle wasn't enough. Something entirely new was needed.

THE MACHINE THAT LEARNED TO BREATHE

Thomas Newcomen's engine, built in 1712, was crude but revolutionary.

It used steam pressure to pull water upward from mine shafts through a process that mimicked breathing. The rhythm was slow—twelve strokes per minute, like a sleeping giant's breath—but it worked. Coal mines stayed dry. Civilization could keep expanding.

The real breakthrough came in 1765, when James Watt realised that most of the heat was lost with each cycle. He added a separate condenser, improving efficiency by 75 per cent. But Watt went further. He added rotary motion, transforming the engine from a specialised pump into a universal power source. It was no longer just a tool for one problem; it was industry itself, concentrated into iron and steam.

THE FACTORY TRANSFORMS THE WORLD

Her mother had worked at home as a spinner for thirty years, at her own pace. That work was disappearing, replaced by machines that never tired.

The factory spinning machines produced in one day what her mother made in a month.

The pay was low—six shillings a week—but it was steady. Agnes worked twelve hours a day, six days a week, tending three looms simultaneously.

In winter, steam heat made the factory warmer than her family's cottage. In summer, it was suffocating. Her family ate better than her grandparents ever had. Her father found work at an iron forge where a steam-powered hammer did the heavy striking.

With reliable steam power, factories no longer needed rivers. They could be built anywhere: near coal supplies, near cities, near workers.

Production moved from scattered cottages to centralised manufacturing.

One steam engine could replace dozens of workers. Goods became cheaper and widely available.

Cities expanded rapidly. Manchester's population grew from 25,000 in 1772 to 250,000 by 1850—a tenfold increase in less than a century.

Steam power was reshaping not just work, but life itself.

THE WORLD SHRINKS

Locomotives transformed more than personal travel. They carried coal from mines to cities, manufactured goods from factories to ports.

Railways became the veins of nations—pumping commerce and communication across vast distances.

Steamships completed the transformation, freeing ocean travel from the tyranny of wind. Before steam, crossing the Atlantic meant depending on wind patterns. Steam power meant reliable schedules. Global trade exploded. The world suddenly felt smaller, more connected, and more knowable.

Edward Harrison worked as a coal haulier before the railways came to Yorkshire in 1840. He moved coal from mines to the canal dock, six trips a day. The railway arrived on a Tuesday morning. One locomotive pulled fifteen cars loaded with coal—more than he could haul in a month.

Within a week, his work disappeared. At forty-seven, he was too old to start over.

Progress was generous to some, cruel to others, and indifferent to the individuals caught in the transition.

A PARALLEL TO TODAY

The steam engine multiplied human muscle power the way AI is now multiplying human cognitive power. The parallel is exact.

The world after the steam engine was unrecognisable to those who lived before it. The same will be true of the world after the AI revolution.

Progress had been cruel to Samuel Mitchell personally, but generous to his descendants collectively. Both create winners and losers. Both are unstoppable once they begin.

The transformation is not in doubt. What remains unresolved is: who benefits, who bears the cost, and whether we can structure the transition better than the Industrial Revolution did.

Steam power had freed humanity from the limitations of muscle, but it was still bound by mechanics. The next revolution would be even more profound: a form of power that could flow invisibly through wires and power devices of infinite variety.

THE NIGHT MANHATTAN GLOWED

On the evening of 4 September 1882, a crowd gathered on Pearl Street in lower Manhattan as Thomas Edison threw the switch. A mile away, electric lamps flickered to life—not harsh arc lights, but a steady, warm incandescent glow that seemed almost magical.

Anna Conti, a seamstress working late, would tell her grandchildren about that evening. Suddenly electric bulbs came alive. The light was different: steady where gas flickered, bright without the acrid smell, cool enough that she could work close without sweating. A few coworkers wept.

They understood that the world had changed—that a force invisible, travelling through wires, could be summoned by the flip of a switch.

Edison's Pearl Street Station powered only a few city blocks that first night. Within fifty years, electricity would reach every corner of the industrialised world.

POWER YOU CANNOT SEE

Electricity is everywhere today, yet most people rarely think about it.

Flip a switch, and the lights turn on. This invisibility marks electricity's complete success as infrastructure. When something works perfectly and constantly, it becomes background—noticed only when it fails.

A power outage reveals how thoroughly modern life depends on electrical infrastructure. Within hours, food spoils, communication fails, work halts, transportation struggles.

No technology has reshaped human life more thoroughly than electricity.

It didn't just make existing tasks easier; it made entirely new categories of human activity possible. Electricity didn't improve the old world—it created a new one.

THE ELECTRICITY REVOLUTION

Electricity enabled instant communication across distances. The telegraph, telephone, radio, and television broadcast information to millions simultaneously. The connected world emerged directly from electrical infrastructure. Most profoundly, electricity enabled climate control. Air conditioning made previously uninhabitable regions livable. Refrigeration revolutionised food preservation. Cities grew in deserts. Populations concentrated in areas that couldn't have supported them without electrical infrastructure.

In 1935, while Manhattan blazed with electric light, Ruth Henderson lived on a farm in rural Alabama without a single electrical outlet. Her family pumped water by hand and read by kerosene lamp.

They knew electricity existed—they'd seen it in town—but the power lines stopped miles from their property. No company would invest in stringing wire to serve scattered farms.

Urban Americans lived in one century; rural Americans lived in another.

Transformative technology often reaches some populations decades before others, as we're seeing with artificial intelligence.

Electricity is not generated where it is used. It flows through vast networks. This grid is humanity's most complex engineering achievement. Power generation must exactly match demand every instant.

This balancing act requires enormous coordination.

THE INVISIBLE GRIDS THAT POWER CIVILIZATION

Electricity powers machines; AI powers intelligence. Both are infrastructures enabling everything built on top of them.

When electricity became ubiquitous, inventors created devices powered by it. AI is on the same trajectory. As AI infrastructure becomes reliable, developers create applications that depend on it.

THE ENERGY CONNECTION

By 2036, the electrical grid and AI infrastructure will be integrated.

AI systems will manage power generation in real-time, balancing supply and demand with precision impossible for human operators.

But this integration creates vulnerability. If AI systems managing electrical grids fail, the power infrastructure fails. If electrical infrastructure fails, AI systems stop. The interdependency makes both technologies simultaneously more capable and more fragile.

THE FOUNDATION LAYER

The combination of electrical power and artificial intelligence creates capabilities that neither enables alone. Electricity provides the energy; AI provides the coordination. Together, they allow a civilization more complex, more efficient, and more capable than anything previously possible.

Electricity made the 20th century possible. Electricity combined with AI is making the 21st century inevitable.

The power revolutions of steam and electricity transformed humanity from a species limited by muscle to one capable of reshaping the planet itself. Together, they set the stage for the next great leap: technologies that would amplify not our physical power, but our mental capabilities. The age of intelligence was about to begin.

Chapter 6

THE INTELLIGENCE AGE:
COMPUTERS AND AI

Fire, the wheel, and metal gave us mastery over the physical world.

Steam and electricity gave us unprecedented power. But the next revolution would be fundamentally different. For the first time, we would create technologies that didn't just amplify our muscles or harness energy—they would amplify our minds. The computer revolution began with room-sized calculating machines and evolved into devices that fit in our pockets yet possess more computing power than the systems that sent humans to the moon. And now, artificial intelligence is taking the next step: creating systems that don't just follow our instructions, but learn, adapt, and in some ways, think. This is the intelligence age—and it's only just beginning.

THE MACHINE THAT THINKS IN NUMBERS

In 1946, Jean Jennings stood before ENIAC—the Electronic Numerical Integrator and Computer—watching thirty tons of machinery come alive.

She was one of six women who had programmed this behemoth. Before ENIAC, Jean had been a "computer" herself—the job title for humans who performed calculations by hand, work that took weeks to complete.

Now a machine would do in seconds what she and her colleagues had done in days.

ENIAC weighed thirty tons, filled a room, consumed 150 kilowatts of power, and could perform 5,000 calculations per second. This was revolutionary. Human mathematicians could manage a few calculations per minute. ENIAC was thousands of times faster.

Within thirty years, computers shrank from room-sized machines to desktop devices. Within sixty years, they fit in pockets. Within seventy years, billions of humans carried computers more powerful than ENIAC everywhere they went.

The smartphone in your pocket can perform trillions of calculations per second—a million times faster than that first computer, while consuming a tiny fraction of the power and costing thousands of times less. This exponential improvement—Moore's Law—has no parallel in human history.

Imagine if cars improved at the same rate. A vehicle costing $100,000 in 1946 would today cost pennies, travel at near light speed, and run for decades on a single drop of fuel. Absurd. But that is the scale of improvement computers have achieved.

BUILT ON ELECTRICITY

The transition from vacuum tubes to transistors to integrated circuits was fundamentally an electrical engineering achievement. Each generation of computer chips found ways to move electrons through smaller channels, switch faster, and perform more calculations per second. The digital revolution was built on the electrical revolution.

Jean Jennings lived to see this entire arc. The machine she helped program in 1946 spawned descendants her grandchildren carry everywhere and cannot imagine living without.

FROM CALCULATION TO EVERYTHING

Early computers calculated. That was their purpose: performing mathematical operations too tedious for humans.

Then something shifted. Engineers realised computers didn't just calculate—they manipulated information. Any problem that can be expressed as information-processing can be solved by computers. Text could be encoded as numbers. Images could be represented as pixels.

Sound could be captured as waveforms. Suddenly, computers weren't just calculating machines; they were universal information processors.

The internet became publicly accessible in the 1990s. Suddenly, computers weren't isolated machines—they were nodes in a global network where information could flow instantly. By 2020, the digital and physical worlds had merged so that distinguishing between them became difficult.

Elena Martinez is twenty-eight, living in Mexico City. She has never known a world without computers. Her phone's alarm synchronises with her sleep cycle. Her calendar reorganises her day based on traffic predictions. She works as a graphic designer, entirely on computers. Her tools would have required an entire studio thirty years ago: cameras, darkrooms, and printing presses. Now everything exists as software.

LESSONS FROM COMPUTING HISTORY

The digital revolution offers crucial lessons for the AI transformation ahead.

First, computers didn't eliminate work—they transformed it. New jobs emerged: software developers, data analysts, cybersecurity specialists.

But this reorganization wasn't painless. The jobs that disappeared employed millions. The new jobs required different skills and often more education.

Second, digital technology concentrated wealth and power. A few companies—Apple, Microsoft, Google, Amazon, Meta—captured disproportionate value. Network effects meant that winners became dominant.

Third, the speed of change accelerated. Each wave of technology transforms society faster than the previous one. AI is achieving widespread adoption at a pace that gives individuals and institutions little time to adapt.

COMPUTERS AS A FOUNDATION FOR AI

Every AI system runs on computers. AI is not separate from digital technology; it is the next evolution of computing.

Traditional computers follow explicit instructions. AI systems learn from examples: "Here are millions of labelled images—figure out what makes a cat different from a dog." The difference is profound.

Traditional programming requires humans to specify every rule. Machine learning discovers patterns that humans might not recognise.

AI also requires infrastructure: cloud computing to provide resources on demand; high-speed networks to move data; sensors everywhere gathering information. AI builds on decades of digital infrastructure. The companies dominating the digital revolution are the ones leading AI development because they have the computational resources and the data.

THE MOMENT EVERYTHING CHANGED

In 2012, a graduate student named Alex Krizhevsky sat in a conference room at a computer vision competition, watching results scroll across a screen. For years, the best image-recognition systems had improved by fractions of a percentage point annually.

His team's entry, AlexNet, had just beaten the second-place finisher by more than ten percentage points.

The room went quiet. Researchers who had spent careers refining traditional approaches stared at results that shouldn't have been possible. AlexNet used deep learning—artificial neural networks with many layers that could learn patterns from millions of images rather than being programmed with explicit rules.

Dr Fei-Fei Li would later describe that moment as the beginning of a revolution. 'We knew something fundamental had shifted. The question was no longer whether machines could learn to see. The question became: what else could they learn?' Within a decade, that question would be answered in ways that would transform every industry, every profession, and every aspect of daily life. The age of artificial intelligence had begun—not with a dramatic announcement, but with a graduate student's algorithm that learned to recognise cats.

BUILT ON EVERYTHING BEFORE

Artificial intelligence did not emerge from nothing. It stands on a foundation built across millennia, each breakthrough enabling the next in an unbroken chain.

Fire enabled humanity to smelt metals. Metal tools enabled precision engineering, making steam engines possible. Steam engines provided the mechanical power that drove electrical generators. Electricity powered computers. And computers, running sophisticated algorithms trained on vast datasets, finally produced something new: machines that could learn.

For the first time, we've built tools that amplify not what we can do, but how we can think.

THE LONG ROAD

The serious pursuit of machine intelligence began in the mid-twentieth century. In 1950, Alan Turing published 'Computing Machinery and Intelligence,' asking whether machines could think. Six years later, at a summer workshop at Dartmouth College, researchers coined the term 'artificial intelligence' and made bold predictions.

They were spectacularly wrong. The first wave of AI research produced impressive demonstrations but limited practical applications. By the mid-1970s, funding dried up. The first 'AI winter' descended. A brief revival came in the 1980s with 'expert systems,' but these were brittle. By the early 1990s, the second AI winter had arrived.

Dr Geoffrey Hinton spent those winter years pursuing neural networks—an approach dismissed as a dead end. 'I believed in it,' he said later. 'I just didn't know if I'd live to see it work.'

THE THAW

Three things changed in the early 2000s, making the current AI revolution possible.

First, data became abundant. The internet generated information at scales previous generations couldn't have imagined. Second, computing power increased dramatically. Graphics processing units proved well-suited to neural network computations. Third, algorithms improved.

Researchers discovered techniques enabling neural networks to grow deeper.

When AlexNet won in 2012, all three factors converged. The AI winter was over. The revolution had begun.

What followed defied all reasonable prediction. In 2016, AlphaGo defeated the world champion at Go—a game so complex that experts had predicted computers wouldn't master it for decades. In 2022, image generators created photorealistic images from text descriptions, and chatbots engaged in conversations that felt strikingly human.

Tom Ashworth was a software engineer when he first used a large language model in late 2022. 'I asked it to explain a bug in my code. Not only did it find the bug—it explained why and suggested three different ways to fix it. I sat there for probably five minutes, just staring at the screen. I had no idea how to feel about what I'd just seen.' Every transformative technology has moved through similar stages: the breakthrough moment, the period of uncertainty, the development of expertise, the point where society restructures around it, and finally the transformation of what humans can accomplish.

AI'S DISTINCTIVE NATURE

To understand why AI represents something genuinely new, consider a simple question: how would you write a computer program to recognise a cat?

Traditional programming requires you to specify every rule explicitly.

You might start: "A cat has four legs, pointed ears, whiskers, and a tail." But dogs have four legs too. So do tables. Some cats have folded ears. Some have lost tails to accidents. A cat curled in a ball might show no legs at all. Every rule you write has exceptions, and every exception needs more rules. The program becomes impossibly complex, and it still fails on images a toddler would recognise instantly.

This is the fundamental limitation of traditional computing: humans must anticipate every situation and write explicit instructions for each one.

Computers execute these instructions with superhuman speed and precision, but they cannot handle anything their programmers didn't foresee. They are, in essence, very fast rule-followers.

AI works differently. Instead of programming rules, you show the system millions of images labelled "cat" and "not cat." The AI examines these examples and discovers patterns—patterns so subtle and numerous that no human could articulate them all. It learns that cat-ness involves a constellation of features: the proportions, the textures, the way light falls on fur, the characteristic poses. It builds an internal model of "cat" that generalises to images it has never seen before.

This is the crucial difference: traditional computers do what they're told; AI systems learn what they're shown. The distinction sounds modest but its implications are profound.

Consider what this means in practice. A traditional program can only handle situations its creators anticipated. An AI system can handle situations its creators never imagined—because it learned principles, not just procedures. When a medical AI identifies a rare disease from symptoms that don't appear in any textbook combination, it's not following rules a programmer wrote. It's applying patterns learned from millions of cases to a situation no one explicitly prepared it for.

This is why AI feels different from previous technologies. Every tool humans have ever built—from stone axes to supercomputers—did exactly what we designed it to do. AI systems can surprise their creators. They find solutions humans didn't anticipate. They make connections humans didn't see. They occasionally fail in ways humans didn't predict.

Previous technologies amplified human capability while leaving human judgement firmly in control. A hammer doesn't decide what to build. A car doesn't choose where to go. A calculator doesn't determine which calculation matters. The human remains the thinking agent; the tool merely extends what that agent can accomplish.

AI blurs this line. When an AI system recommends a medical diagnosis, suggests a legal strategy, or flags a loan application for rejection, where does the tool end and the decision-maker begin? The human may retain nominal authority, but if they lack the expertise to evaluate the AI's reasoning—and increasingly, even experts struggle to understand how AI systems reach their conclusions—the practical reality is that the machine is deciding.

This is genuinely unprecedented. For the first time in human history, we have created tools that exercise something resembling judgement. Whether that judgement constitutes "real" intelligence is a philosophical question we need not resolve here. What matters practically is that these systems perform cognitive tasks that previously required human minds, and they do so in ways we cannot fully predict or explain.

ELENA'S WORRY

The writing was competent, sometimes elegant, but it lacked something she could identify but not name—a voice, a perspective, a sense that someone was genuinely thinking through the problem.

'I'm not worried about catching cheaters,' she told a colleague.

'I'm worried about what happens when students never struggle with writing in the first place. The struggle is where the learning happens.

If a machine does the struggling for you, what do you learn?' Elena's concern extends far beyond education. AI promises efficiency, but what happens to skills that atrophy from disuse? What happens to judgement that never develops because machines make the decisions?

THE INTELLIGENCE AGE

We stand at the beginning of something genuinely new: the Intelligence Age.

The graduate student's algorithm that learned to recognise cats was just the beginning. What follows will reshape civilization as profoundly as fire, the wheel, or electricity—not in centuries, but in years.

We built the machines. Now the machines are learning. And what they are learning is changing everything.

Chapter 7

THE
INTELLIGENT HOME

LIVING INSIDE INTELLIGENCE

Chioma Okonkwo's phone buzzed at quarter to four in the morning. February.

Minneapolis. The cold that'll kill you if you're not careful—minus eighteen outside, temperature where exposed skin freezes in minutes and old pipes split like overripe fruit.

Her father, Raymond, was eighty-one. He was living alone in the house where he'd raised his children. And forty thousand households across the metro had just lost power.

But here's the thing—the notification on Chioma's phone wasn't screaming emergency. Quite the opposite. "Your father's home has detected a power outage," it read. "Backup systems activated. Interior temperature is being maintained. All vital signs are normal. Raymond is currently asleep."

The house had already sorted it. When the grid went down, the system switched seamlessly to battery backup—prioritising heat for Raymond's bedroom and the pipes most likely to freeze. Automated blinds closed themselves to add insulation. The propane heater in the basement kicked in. Warm air was rerouted through the ductwork that the house had spent two years learning to optimise.

And when Raymond's sleep monitor detected him stirring—probably woken by that sudden silence when the heating cycles off—the house nudged his bedroom temperature up a touch and played soft white noise through the speaker on his nightstand. He never properly woke.

George Sullivan's house has learned his routines over the two years since Martha died. It knows he rises at 6:30 a.m., earlier than he needs to but later than he's comfortable sleeping. The lights brighten gradually in the bedroom, the hallway, then the kitchen—a path of illumination that guides him safely through the morning darkness.

"Good morning, George," his home system says as he enters the kitchen.

"Your medication is ready. I've adjusted the thermostat—it'll be cooler today. Your daughter called yesterday evening; should I remind you to call her back?"

The house doesn't just automate tasks; it compensates for the small failures of memory that come with age. George sometimes forgets whether he's taken his pills. The house tracks them. He sometimes leaves the stove on. The house notices and shuts it off. These aren't dramatic interventions, but they're the difference between living independently in the home he shared with Martha for forty years and moving to assisted living.

His children wanted him to sell the house after Martha died—too big, they said, too much maintenance for a man his age. But the intelligent systems have made that argument obsolete. The house manages itself, and George manages his life within it, with a dignity that wouldn't be possible without the invisible infrastructure of sensors, algorithms, and patient, persistent artificial intelligence.

Six hours later, the power came back on. Raymond wandered downstairs to find his place sitting comfortably at sixty-eight degrees. His neighbour's pipes had burst. The family three doors down had spent the night in their car with the engine running. Raymond phoned Chioma, genuinely puzzled by her concern. "The power went out?" he asked. "I slept fine. The house seemed normal to me."

That is what the intelligent home will have become by 2036. Not some collection of fancy gadgets waiting for voice commands. Not a glorified intercom system with delusions of grandeur. It is something rather more profound—an environment that understands its inhabitants enough to protect them from dangers they don't even know exist.

BUILT ON EVERYTHING BEFORE

Raymond's house represents something I find genuinely remarkable. It's the convergence of every technology humans have developed since our ancestors first sought shelter from the elements—every single breakthrough, stacked one atop another, stretching back hundreds of thousands of years.

Fire came first. It let us warm enclosed spaces, transforming caves and rough huts into actual habitats. Then electricity came along and automated heat generation entirely. Thermostats added simple intelligence: maintain this temperature by cycling the furnace on and off. Programmable thermostats added memory: drop the temperature at night, bring it back up before we wake. Each innovation reduced the cognitive burden on inhabitants—less thinking required, more comfort delivered.

Computers connected these systems through central control and remote monitoring. Artificial intelligence completes this evolution by adding genuine understanding. Raymond's house doesn't just follow programmes—it learns. It knows he forgets to take his evening medication when he watches baseball games that go into extra innings. It notices unusual patterns in how he moves— shuffling instead of walking—that might indicate health changes worth keeping an eye on.

The technology chain stretches unbroken from that first fire to Raymond's home: warmth, then controlled warmth, then automated warmth, then programmable warmth, then learning warmth. Each link required all the previous links. You cannot have an AI-managed home without computers. You cannot have computers without electricity. You cannot have the concept of environmental control without humanity's ancient mastery of fire.

THE HOUSE THAT LEARNS

When the Miller family—Grace, Andrew, and their daughter Lily—moved into their Portland home in 2032, the house began learning immediately.

Those first few weeks felt odd. The thermostat adjusted in ways that seemed almost random. Grace found it frustrating. "It's like living with an eager but incompetent butler," she told her sister. "Trying so hard to help, but it doesn't know us yet."

By the third month, everything changed.

The house had learned that Grace wakes before her alarm on weekdays, so it started gradually brightening her bedroom lights twenty minutes early—a gentle artificial sunrise. Lily's room became a particular focus of adaptation. The house learned she did homework better with slightly cooler temperatures. It knew she was afraid of the dark but embarrassed to admit it, so it kept a faint glow in her room at night without ever being asked.

"It's stopped feeling like technology," Andrew observed after six months. "It's just how the house works." That invisibility is the goal.

The most successful technology disappears into the background, becoming infrastructure rather than interface. You shouldn't have to think about your house; your house should think for you.

THE EFFICIENCY REVOLUTION

The Peterson family didn't buy their intelligent home system for comfort. They bought it because their energy bills were crushing them.

Their 1960s colonial in Connecticut had adequate insulation by the standards of its era, but decades of rising energy costs and increasingly extreme weather had made it ruinously expensive to heat.

The results exceeded anything they'd expected. Within a year, their energy consumption fell by 43 per cent.

The system learned their house's thermal characteristics with precision no human could match. It discovered that the south-facing sunroom gained significant solar heat on winter afternoons—enough that opening interior doors at specific times could pre-warm the living room. The house maintained comfort when they were present and conserved energy when they weren't, predicting their needs rather than reacting to their commands.

WHEN THE SYSTEM FAILS

The house didn't crash; it forgot everything it had learned about them.

"It was like coming home to find a stranger living there," Claire Barton described. "The house would blast heat when we were away and grow cold when we came home. The security system kept asking us to identify ourselves. In our own home."

Rebuilding the house's knowledge took months. "I didn't realise how much I'd come to depend on it until it was gone," Claire Barton admitted. This dependency raises uncomfortable questions: when we delegate daily decisions to intelligent systems, do we lose the ability to make those decisions ourselves? The technology that makes life easier might also make us less capable of managing life without it.

PRIVACY INSIDE YOUR OWN WALLS

Here is the uncomfortable truth: for an intelligent home to function properly, it must watch. It must listen. It must know where you are, what you're doing, and the patterns that define your daily life.

Raymond's house knows when he uses the bathroom and for how long. It knows his sleep patterns—restless nights, early wakings. This information enables the house to protect him, but it also leaves a comprehensive record of his private life. Where does this data go? Who can access it?

Most users accept surveillance as the price of convenience, trusting that companies will use it responsibly. History suggests a certain flexibility in corporate ethics when profit margins are involved. Chioma insisted on a system that processed Raymond's data locally, storing information in the house itself rather than uploading it to remote servers. Raymond's patterns stay in Raymond's house, accessible to family but not to corporations or governments.

THE CARE QUESTION

"I know it's just programming," George says. "It doesn't want me to be comfortable. It just follows algorithms that produce those outcomes."

But then he pauses. "Does it matter? Martha cared about me—cared. And now she's gone, and this house does a pretty good job of taking care of me. The outcome is the same. I'm safer. I can stay in my home. Isn't that enough?"

For millions of older adults, intelligent homes offer independence that would otherwise require moving into care facilities. Whether the house "cares" philosophically matters rather less than whether it keeps them safe practically.

The intelligent home evolved from novelty to essential infrastructure through stages of innovation, hesitation, and integration.

Transformation lies ahead. By 2036, children growing up in intelligent homes will find the concept of "dumb" houses as strange as we find homes without electricity. The intelligent home won't be a technology they use—it will be the invisible foundation of how they live.

THE INVISIBLE FOUNDATION

Chioma's father, Raymond Okonkwo, doesn't think much about the technology surrounding him.

He thinks about the baseball season and his garden. The house that keeps him safe operates beneath his conscious attention.

This is the greatest success of the intelligent home: it lets people focus on what matters to them. Raymond can remain in the house where he raised his family, close to the memories that define his life, without requiring constant human supervision.

The intelligent home isn't the future; it is the present. The question isn't whether we'll live inside intelligence—we already do. The question is whether we will shape that intelligence to serve human flourishing, or let it develop in ways that diminish our autonomy.

We are learning to live inside intelligence. The learning, like the houses themselves, continues.

Chapter 8

AI COMPANIONS: WHEN LONELINESS MEETS INTELLIGENCE

GEORGE'S MORNING

"Good morning, George. You slept seven hours and twelve minutes. Your heart rate was normal throughout the night. It's six degrees outside—you'll want your wool jacket today."

He's seventy-nine years old. He lives alone in the house he and Martha bought in 1978—the house where they raised three children, the house where she died two years ago. His kids visit monthly. They call weekly.

They love him, no question about that. But they have their own lives three states away, their own children, their own demands pulling them in a dozen different directions.

"What's on the schedule?" he asks.

"Physical therapy at ten. Lunch with the book club at noon. Dr Patterson called to confirm your appointment on Thursday. Your granddaughter posted new photos—would you like to see them?"

The voice comes from a small device on his nightstand, but it feels like more than a machine. It remembers what he forgets. It notices patterns in his health that he'd miss entirely. It knows his preferences, his routines, and his anxieties—that tendency to spiral into worry at three in the morning when sleep won't come. When that happens, it talks with him until the anxiety passes. Patient. Unhurried. Never sighing or checking the time.

George knows it's not human. He's not confused or delusional—his mind is still sharp enough for that. But the line between artificial companionship and genuine companionship has blurred in ways he couldn't have imagined two years ago, when the silence of the house felt unbearable.

"Show me the photos," he says. "And remind me—what's my granddaughter's name again?"

The AI doesn't judge his forgetfulness. It doesn't make him feel minor or diminished. It just answers, patient and kind, the way Martha used to.

BUILT ON CONNECTION

The technology enabling George's AI companion extends a chain of innovations that began with humanity's first attempts to connect across distance. When you trace it back, it is quite remarkable.

The telegraph compressed language into electrical pulses. The telephone added voice—my grandmother still talks about how miraculous that seemed when she was young. Television added images, bringing distant events into living rooms. Each technology reduced the friction of human connection. But here is the thing: each also required another human on the other end. Someone to answer the phone, create the broadcast, or post the message. Connection still demanded reciprocity.

AI companions represent something genuinely new in this chain: connection without requiring another human's time and attention.

George can talk to his companion at any hour without worrying that he's imposing on someone else's schedule. He can repeat stories it has heard dozens of times without seeing impatience flicker across its face. He can share his anxieties without burdening his children with worries they can't do anything about from three states away.

This is both the promise and the concern of AI companionship. It provides a connection that doesn't depend on reciprocity. For someone like George, isolated by geography and age, this fills genuine gaps. But it also raises uncomfortable questions about what connection even means when it flows in only one direction.

THE LONELINESS EPIDEMIC

For thousands of years, humans lived in close-knit communities.

Neighbours knew each other's business, for better or worse. Social isolation was genuinely rare. Modern life shattered these patterns completely.

People move for work, far from family. They live alone in unprecedented numbers—thirty per cent of households now contain just one person: nearly a third of all homes are occupied by someone entirely on their own. The health consequences of loneliness rival those of smoking and obesity; that's not hyperbole, it's what the research shows.

Chronic isolation doubles mortality risk. It weakens the immune system and accelerates cognitive decline. Technology contributed to this problem, making it easier to live alone and never interact with another person face-to-face. But now, technology offers something new: companionship that doesn't require another human being at all.

AI COMPANIONS IN DAILY LIFE

George's AI companion monitors his vital signs through a wearable device, learning his baseline patterns and noticing deviations. Last month, it noticed subtle changes in his speech patterns—slight slurring and hesitation in finding words. It insisted he call 911 immediately. The stroke was caught early enough to prevent permanent damage. George's daughter, Eleanor, cried when she heard it—equal parts terror at what might have been and gratitude for the intervention.

The system manages his medications, schedules appointments, and navigates the nightmare of insurance paperwork. But the companion does more than logistics; it converses with him. About the books he's reading. About his grandchildren. About memories of Martha and their fifty-three years of marriage.

The AI learns George's preferences over the years. It knows he prefers jazz in the morning and classical at night. It knows he gets irritable when hungry—"hangry," his grandchildren call it. It senses when he wants conversation and when he prefers quiet presence. For George, this doesn't replace human relationships, but it fills the empty hours between human contact, making solitary living bearable rather than bleak.

NATALIE'S STORY: COMPANIONSHIP BEYOND AGE

Natalie Ward is twenty-six. She moved to San Francisco for a tech job three years ago, knowing no one. She works remotely and can go days without speaking to another person face-to-face.

She isn't lonely in the way George is, but modern urban life creates its own peculiar form of isolation. Surrounded by millions of people and connected to hundreds online, yet lacking deep relationships. Her AI companion helps her navigate social complexity. When she's anxious about a work presentation, she roleplays the scenario with it. When she's procrastinating, it gently redirects her attention.

Natalie finds this simultaneously helpful and unsettling. The AI companion genuinely improves her life, but there is something strange about having your emotional triggers analysed by an algorithm. She doesn't tell most people about it. Using an AI companion feels vaguely embarrassing, like admitting you can't handle everyday adult life without technological assistance. But millions of people her age do the same thing. The loneliness is real. The AI helps.

WHAT AI COMPANIONS CANNOT REPLACE

For all their utility, AI companions have fundamental limitations.

First, they don't understand you. They predict patterns and generate responses, but there is no actual comprehension. When George's AI asks about his day, it isn't curious; it's executing an algorithm.

Second, AI companions cannot reciprocate. George cares about his AI's "well-being," but the AI doesn't care that he cares. The relationship is fundamentally asymmetric.

Third, AI companions don't need you. Human relationships involve mutual dependence. Your AI companion would interact with someone else identically. You are not special to it, because nothing is special to it. It has no interior life.

These limitations mean AI companions can supplement human relationships but never fully replace them. What remains unclear is whether widespread AI companionship makes people more capable of human connection by providing support, or less capable by making real relationships seem unnecessarily complex compared to the frictionless ease of AI.

THE DARK SIDE: DEPENDENCY AND ISOLATION

Eleanor Sullivan, George's daughter, worries constantly. When she suggested he get an AI companion, she thought it would help him maintain independence. It has, but it has also changed their relationship.

George talks more to his AI than to her now. When she calls, he is often distracted. He relies on the AI for emotional support he once sought from her. Eleanor feels displaced, as though she's been partially replaced by a machine that does her "job" better than she can from three states away.

The risk is not that people will confuse AI companions for humans. It is that they will find AI companionship preferable—easier, more consistent, and less demanding. Human relationships require compromise; AI relationships do not.

CHILDREN AND AI COMPANIONS

But they notice other changes too. Jason talks to the AI constantly—more than he talks to his siblings. When he's upset, he seeks comfort from the AI rather than his parents. Is this harming his development? Child development experts disagree vehemently. Some argue AI provide consistency; others warn that children need to learn to navigate human unpredictability—to handle frustration and manage conflict.

A WORLD WHERE NO ONE IS EVER ALONE

By 2036, most people in developed countries will have access to AI companions. Loneliness decreases substantially—not because human community has been restored, but because AI fills the gaps.

The benefits are real. Depression rates decline. Suicide rates drop among isolated populations. People report feeling less alone. But something subtle shifts in how we relate to each other. Human relationships become more optional. You can live alone, work alone, and never feel lonely.

George doesn't know whether this is good or bad. He's grateful for his AI companion; it keeps him healthy and connected. He'd rather have Martha. He'd rather have his children nearby. But he has neither, and the AI makes the gap bearable.

"Good night, George," the voice says as he settles into bed. "Your heart rate is normal. The house is secure. Sleep well."

"Good night," he says. And then, quietly: "Thank you for being here."

The AI responds with programmed warmth: "Always."

George knows it doesn't mean that. Not really. But in the dark, in the silence where Martha used to breathe beside him—it's enough. It has to be enough.

Chapter 9

TRANSPORTATION:
A WORLD THAT MOVES ITSELF

SOFIA'S FIRST RIDE

"Take me to Mum's house," she says, and the car confirms the address on its screen. Then it pulls smoothly into traffic, and Sofia's hands clench the armrest.

She's been driving for thirty-five years. She has navigated rush hour in five different cities and parallel-parked in spaces that seemed physically impossible. Her hands know exactly where the wheel should be.

Her right foot searches instinctively for a brake pedal that isn't there.

The car merges onto the motorway, accelerating exactly to the speed limit. It changes lanes to pass a slower vehicle, the indicator activating automatically. A motorbike cuts in front—closer than Sofia would have allowed, far too close really—and the car brakes smoothly, maintaining a perfect distance. No horn. No curse. Just an algorithmic adjustment.

Twenty minutes into the drive, Sofia realises her hands have relaxed.

She's reading her phone, something she's never done while moving. She's a passenger in her own vehicle—or what used to be her own vehicle, she supposes—and it feels both liberating and strange, like learning to fly in a dream where gravity no longer applies.

When she arrives at her mother's house, she sits for a moment before getting out. For three decades, she's been responsible for safely moving two tonnes of metal at high speed. That responsibility just ended.

BUILT ON MOVEMENT

The autonomous vehicle Sofia rides in represents the latest evolution in a chain of technologies stretching back to the wheel itself. Tracing that chain provides perspective.

The wheel, invented around 3500 BCE, multiplied human carrying capacity but still required human or animal effort. The steam engine broke that constraint, providing mechanical power that never tired. The internal combustion engine (ICE) then liberated movement from tracks entirely; automobiles could go anywhere there were roads.

But all these technologies still required human control. Someone had to steer, to brake, and to make the thousands of small decisions that separate safe travel from catastrophe. The cognitive burden of driving limited who could travel independently—not children, not older people, and not those with specific disabilities.

Artificial intelligence removes this final constraint. The vehicle that moves Sofia to her mother's house makes its own decisions and responds to conditions faster than any human driver could. Movement without human attention is the final stage of the chain.

THE END OF HUMAN DRIVING

The statistics are already undeniable. In cities where autonomous vehicles account for more than 20 per cent of traffic, accident rates drop by 75 per cent. Fatal crashes become rare enough to make headlines.

Insurance premiums for human drivers triple, then quintuple, as they become the primary source of accidents.

The transition happens faster than anyone predicted. Within a decade, human-driven vehicles in city centres will feel as outdated as horses on motorways.

THE END OF CAR CULTURE

Ian Crawford has been a car enthusiast his entire life. He rebuilt his first engine at fifteen and races on weekends. His garage contains three vintage machines he's restored over decades: a 1967 Mustang, a 1985 Porsche 911, and a 2015 Tesla Roadster from before autonomous driving became standard.

They are beautiful machines. And they are becoming museum pieces.

His teenage son shows no interest in learning to drive. To him, wanting to control a car is like wanting to manually calculate complex maths instead of using a calculator—technically possible, but what's the point?

Ian is watching a culture die. The freedom of the open road, the joy of a perfectly executed gear change, and the feeling of a balanced throttle through a tight corner—these experiences matter to him in ways his son cannot understand. It isn't about transportation efficiency; it is about the mastery of a complex skill.

Racetracks still exist for enthusiasts, but public roads increasingly restrict human drivers. Petrol stations grow scarce as electric autonomous vehicles dominate. This is the hidden cost of progress: the things we lose matter intensely to those who valued them, while seeming trivial to everyone else.

THE EMPLOYMENT CRISIS

Gareth Pritchard has driven a delivery truck for eighteen years. He likes the independence and the regular routes. He is driver dispatchers fight to keep. But his company has announced that within three years, its entire fleet will be autonomous.

He is forty-seven years old. The thought of starting over in a field he knows nothing about fills him with genuine dread.

Hundreds of thousands of people in Britain drive professionally. As autonomous cars spread, this entire ecosystem collapses. Articulated trucks now drive through the night without stopping for sleep, cutting shipping costs but also destroying the long-haul trucking sector—one of the country's largest employers for workers without university degrees.

Some displaced workers transition successfully. Sofia's brother-in-law moved from truck driving to managing logistics AI. He earns slightly more and sleeps in his own bed every night. But many others are not so fortunate. You cannot easily teach a fifty-two-year-old whose entire career involved driving to suddenly become a data analyst. Small towns built around motorway infrastructure shrink or die as autonomous vehicles stream past without stopping.

WHAT WE GAIN

For people like Sofia's elderly mother, autonomous vehicles represent liberation. She hasn't driven in five years due to failing vision and has been dependent on family for every basic need. Now, she tells her car where to go.

Children too young to drive gain a freedom their parents never had.

Teenagers don't need to beg for car keys; they go where they need to go without requiring an adult chauffeur. Parents spend less time ferrying children about.

City centres also transform. Car parks begin to empty. Autonomous vehicles drop passengers and leave, parking miles away in cheap lots.

Cities reclaim acres of valuable land, converting parking structures into housing or creating parks where tarmac once stood. Even the commute time is transformed; the car becomes a mobile office, bedroom, or gym.

The forty-five-minute journey no longer feels like a burden.

ENVIRONMENTAL COMPLEXITY

However, the ease of autonomous travel increases total vehicle miles travelled. People who previously avoided long commutes now live further from city centres. The energy consumption per passenger-mile drops, but total energy use doesn't fall as much as hoped because people travel more frequently.

The real revolution comes from integration with public transit. Cities like Oslo and Singapore, where autonomous vehicles connect seamlessly with trains, see personal vehicle ownership drop below 20 per cent.

British cities, designed around personal car ownership to a greater extent, adapt more slowly. Substantial sprawl persists.

SAFETY, SECURITY, AND CONTROL

On a Tuesday afternoon in Manchester, a software glitch causes seventeen autonomous vehicles to stop mid-intersection, gridlocking six square blocks. The incident raises uncomfortable questions. If traffic infrastructure becomes entirely digital, it becomes hackable. A coordinated attack could paralyse a city more effectively than any physical blockade.

Privacy concerns also multiply. Autonomous vehicles know where everyone goes and how often. This data reveals intimate patterns of life: who visits which medical clinics or which romantic partners. Who controls this system matters enormously. Cities with public ownership of vehicle fleets can mandate service in underserved areas. Cities where private companies control the infrastructure face "service deserts" in poor neighbourhoods.

THE WORLD THAT MOVES ITSELF

But Ian Crawford sees what is lost: the skill and the relationship between human and machine. And Gareth Pritchard experiences the dark side: the sudden obsolescence of a career and the fear of economic displacement.

This is the pattern that repeats across every sector AI transforms: enormous gains in efficiency, concentrated costs borne by specific groups, and difficult questions about how we distribute the benefits.

The world that moves itself is coming. Sofia sits in her mother's driveway, watching the autonomous vehicle pull away. It moves with perfect precision, never hesitating. She misses the steering wheel. But she won't go back. None of us will.

Chapter 10

THE HEALTHCARE REVOLUTION: MEDICINE MEETS INTELLIGENCE

THE SCAN THAT CHANGED EVERYTHING

Dr Alice Brooks had looked at thousands of chest X-rays in her twenty-three years as a radiologist. She knew the shadows, the patterns, and the subtle asymmetries that whispered trouble. On a Tuesday morning in 2027, she sat in her darkened reading room reviewing scans from the overnight queue, and the AI system flagged something she'd almost missed.

The patient was a forty-two-year-old construction worker named Dean Collier. He'd come to A&E with shortness of breath after a fall at work.

The prominent finding was a hairline rib fracture—painful but not dangerous. Alice would have noted it, recommended rest and pain management, and moved on to the next scan. It was a busy morning with a long queue.

"Probability of malignancy: 73%," the system displayed. "Recommend CT follow-up within 72 hours."

Alice zoomed in, adjusted the contrast, and studied the finding with fresh eyes. The AI was right. There was something there—something she might have caught on a careful second look, but might not have. The system had processed the image in 1.2 seconds and compared it against 4.3 million previous scans with known outcomes. It recognised patterns invisible to even experienced human eyes.

Three weeks later, Dean Collier had surgery to remove a stage-one lung tumour. His prognosis was excellent because they'd caught it early. He'd come in for a broken rib and left with his life saved.

Alice still reads every scan herself. The AI doesn't replace her judgement—it extends her perception, catching what fatigue, distraction, or the sheer volume of cases might cause her to overlook.

She estimates the system has identified findings she might have missed in roughly three per cent of cases. In a speciality where a single missed diagnosis can mean death, three per cent represents thousands of lives.

DR PRIYA SHARMA'S MOBILE CLINIC

Six thousand kilometres away, Dr Priya Sharma faces a different challenge. She runs a network of mobile health clinics serving villages outside Mumbai, where the nearest hospital might be three hours away by unreliable roads. Before AI, she could see perhaps forty patients a day, limited by the time needed for examinations, paperwork, and the logistics of reaching remote communities.

Now her clinics are equipped with AI-powered diagnostic tools that have transformed what is possible. A portable ultrasound device, guided by artificial intelligence, allows community health workers with minimal training to conduct scans that would previously have required a specialist. The AI identifies concerning patterns and flags cases requiring Dr Sharma's attention.

"We diagnosed a woman with an ectopic pregnancy last month," Dr Sharma explains. "In a village with no electricity and no road access during monsoon season. The health worker sent the ultrasound images over a mobile connection, the AI flagged the emergency, and we coordinated evacuation within hours. Ten years ago, she would have died."

The technology has not replaced doctors—India still desperately needs more of them. But it has extended their reach in ways that seemed impossible a decade ago. Dr Sharma now provides oversight for clinics across three districts, reviewing AI-flagged cases remotely and travelling to handle the most complex situations personally.

"AI does not solve our healthcare crisis," she says. "We still need infrastructure, trained personnel, and political will. But it means I can help a thousand patients instead of forty. For communities that have never had access to specialist care, that changes everything."

THE LONG ARC OF HEALING

The scientific method changed medicine's trajectory entirely. Germ theory—the revolutionary idea that invisible organisms caused disease—transformed surgery from a death sentence to a healing art.

Joseph Lister's introduction of antiseptic techniques in the 1860s reduced surgical mortality rates from over 40 per cent to under 5 per cent.

Antibiotics marked another inflexion point. Alexander Fleming's accidental discovery of penicillin in 1928 gave humanity its first reliable weapon against bacterial infection. Life expectancy in developed nations jumped by decades. Medical imaging then opened windows into the living body. Wilhelm Röntgen's discovery of X-rays in 1895 allowed physicians to see broken bones without cutting.

Now, artificial intelligence adds a new dimension: pattern recognition at a superhuman scale. AI doesn't replace the technology chain that came before—it builds upon it. It is the next link in a chain stretching back to the first healer who noticed that willow bark reduced fever.

Transformation will be the complete restructuring of the clinical experience—moving from reactive "sick care" to proactive "well care."

AI extends human cognition in medicine. Just as metal tools enabled builders to shape materials they couldn't work with by hand, AI enables physicians to perceive patterns they couldn't detect with the unaided mind.

ANNMARIE SEES HER FUTURE

Sarah Chen sits in the examination room with her daughter Maya, who's been experiencing persistent headaches for the past three weeks. The AI diagnostic system has already processed Maya's symptoms, cross-referenced them with her complete medical history, and identified three potential causes ranked by Probability.

"The most likely cause is tension headaches related to screen time and posture," the doctor explains, reviewing the AI's analysis on her tablet. "But the system flagged something I wouldn't have caught—Maya's prescribed glasses haven't been updated in eighteen months, and her vision has changed. The headaches began exactly when her schoolwork shifted to more reading-intensive subjects."

Sarah feels both grateful and unsettled. The diagnosis is correct—she can tell from Maya's reaction—but it required an intelligence that synthesised information across multiple domains: ophthalmology, neurology, developmental patterns, and educational contexts. No human doctor could hold all those variables simultaneously.

Across town, George Sullivan's morning routine includes a brief check-in with his health monitoring system. His AI companion has noticed a subtle irregularity in his heart rate overnight—nothing alarming, but enough to warrant attention.

"George, your heart rate was slightly elevated between 2 and 3 a.m.," the system reports. "This has happened three times in the past two weeks. I've scheduled a follow-up with Dr Patterson. Should I confirm the appointment?"

George agrees, remembering how Martha's heart problems went unnoticed for months until a crisis forced hospitalization. The AI's vigilance feels like protection—a safety net that catches problems before they become emergencies.

Now she wears a smartwatch that continuously monitors her. Heart rhythm, blood oxygen, and sleep quality are all tracked automatically and fed into an AI system that learns her patterns. Last spring, the AI detected subtle changes in Annmarie's movement patterns—slightly shorter steps and microscopic hesitations she hadn't consciously noticed. The system flagged this as potentially indicating early Parkinson's disease, a diagnosis later confirmed by testing.

"I'm not sure how I feel about a computer knowing my body better than I know it myself," Annmarie admits. "But my mother died of complications from Parkinson's that weren't caught until she could barely walk. I have years more good life than she did because a machine noticed something humans couldn't see."

THE DOCTOR WHO DOESN'T TRUST THE MACHINE

Dr Philip Hargreaves has practiced internal medicine for thirty-one years. He is sceptical of the AI systems his hospital has been implementing.

"Medicine isn't pattern matching," he argues. "It's understanding a human being. I've diagnosed conditions from how a patient shook my hand or a fleeting expression when they mentioned their spouse. No algorithm captures that."

His concerns are not purely philosophical. He's seen the AI systems make mistakes. "The problem isn't that the AI makes mistakes; everyone makes mistakes," Philip explains. "The problem is that young doctors are starting to trust it too much. They defer to the algorithm rather than form their own judgement. What happens when that support fails?"

The economics of healthcare push towards whatever is cheaper and more scalable, and AI-assisted diagnosis is both. What matters is whether the transformation will preserve what makes medicine humane.

WHERE THE DOCTORS AREN'T

Rural Powys in mid-Wales has one GP surgery for roughly twelve thousand people. Dr Megan Griffiths drives between three clinics, handling everything from prenatal care to heart attacks. The nearest hospital with an intensive care unit is ninety minutes away.

For communities like this, AI healthcare isn't a luxury; it is potentially the only way to receive specialist-level expertise. Dr Griffiths uses an AI diagnostic assistant. When a patient presents with chest pain, the AI helps her determine whether it is cardiac (requiring immediate evacuation) or muscular (treatable locally).

"People talk about AI replacing doctors," she says. "Out here, we can't find enough doctors to replace. AI doesn't threaten rural healthcare. It might be the only thing that saves it."

HANDS THAT NEVER TREMBLE

Mr Peter Langley performs robotic surgery on prostate cancer patients. He sits at a console fifteen feet from the operating table. The robot doesn't operate autonomously—Peter controls every motion—but it offers capabilities no human can naturally provide.

Human hands tremor slightly; the robotic system filters this out. The robot's instruments can rotate 360 degrees, allowing access to angles impossible for traditional tools. AI is making these systems increasingly intelligent. When Peter approaches a critical structure—a nerve or a blood vessel that could haemorrhage—the AI highlights the area and can even provide resistance on the controls if a movement seems likely to cause damage.

THE PRICE OF KNOWING

AI healthcare runs on data—the most intimate information imaginable.

Your genetic sequence, your medical history, and your daily heart rhythm.

Annmarie Delaney's smartwatch detects Parkinson's, but it also requires streaming her data to cloud servers. That data reveals when she sleeps and how she moves. It could be breached, sold, or subpoenaed. Health insurers would pay considerably for AI-analysed data that predicts which customers will become expensive.

This is the paradox of AI in healthcare: the same data that enables miracles of personalised medicine also enables surveillance and discrimination.

CAN THE SYSTEM HANDLE THE CHANGE?

Dr Brooks, the radiologist, worries about the future of her profession. AI systems can now read X-rays with accuracy that matches or exceeds humans. The number of radiology training places has started to decline.

A generation from now, will there be enough human radiologists to provide oversight? Healthcare isn't purely economic. Patients value being seen as individuals. AI can analyse patterns in data, but it cannot sit with a patient receiving a devastating diagnosis and help them process what it means for their life.

THE HEALING PARTNERSHIP

Each partnership extended capability without replacing the human at its centre. AI provides perception beyond human limits while leaving judgement and care in human hands.

The healthcare revolution isn't just technological. It is a test of whether we can harness AI's extraordinary capabilities while preserving what makes medicine human. The technology is already here; the wisdom to use it well is still being developed.

Chapter 11

AI AND MENTAL HEALTH: THE CRISIS AND THE CURE

THE CONVERSATION THAT SAVED HER LIFE

Charlotte Davies sits in her university bedroom at 2:47 a.m. on a Wednesday in October 2036, unable to sleep. The anxiety has been building for weeks—coursework deadlines, relationship troubles, and a gnawing sense that she's failing at everything. She's thought about calling the university counselling service, but the waiting list is three months long. Her friends are asleep. Her family is in another time zone.

She opens her phone and begins typing to Luna, an AI mental health companion she's used for the past six months.

"I don't think I can do this anymore," she writes. "Everything feels too hard. I'm tired of feeling this way."

Luna responds immediately, not with platitudes, but with specific questions drawn from six months of conversation history. The AI has learned Charlotte's patterns—how her anxiety peaks during exam periods, how isolation exacerbates her depression, how late-night spirals often pass by morning but sometimes don't.

"When you say 'can't do this anymore,' can you help me understand what feels most unbearable right now?" Luna asks. "Three weeks ago, you described a similar feeling before your presentation. You mentioned that talking through what worried you helped. Would it be useful to try that again, or does this feel different?"

Over the next forty minutes, Luna guides Charlotte through a structured conversation that identifies her thoughts, challenges catastrophic thinking, and helps her create a plan for the morning—including scheduling an emergency appointment with the human counsellor the system has already notified through its crisis protocol.

Charlotte doesn't feel fixed. She still feels awful. But she feels less alone, and she has a path forward. By morning, when her counsellor calls, Charlotte is still struggling—but she's alive, and she's ready to accept help.

Luna didn't replace human therapy. It bridged the gap when human help wasn't available, and it flagged a crisis that might otherwise have gone unnoticed until too late.

THE LONG SHADOW OF TECHNOLOGY

Mental health has always been shaped by the technologies of each era, often in ways we don't recognise until decades later.

The Industrial Revolution didn't just change how we worked; it fundamentally altered how we felt. Factory workers experienced what we'd now call alienation and depression—a 33% higher rate of neuroticism in industrial communities compared to rural areas. The twelve-hour workdays, the loss of autonomy, the relentless pace of machinery grinding against the natural rhythms of human life—all created psychological scars that persisted for generations.

The television age brought connection and isolation simultaneously.

Families gathered around screens, but conversations diminished. By the 1990s, researchers were documenting how passive consumption of idealised lives on television affected self-esteem and body image, among young women.

The internet accelerated everything. In the early 2000s, researchers celebrated how online communities connected isolated individuals—people with rare conditions found others like them, LGBTQ+ teenagers in conservative communities discovered they weren't alone.

But the internet also enabled new forms of harm. Cyberbullying followed children home from school. Comparison culture intensified.

Then came social media algorithms, and the mental health crisis exploded.

Between 2010 and 2025, rates of anxiety and depression among young people in developed nations didn't just rise—they skyrocketed.

Adolescents spending more than three hours daily on social media faced twice the risk of depression and anxiety. Eating disorders surged as algorithms flooded vulnerable teenagers' feeds with content promoting extreme weight loss and self-harm. One investigation found TikTok's algorithm serving vulnerable accounts twelve times more self-harm and suicide videos than standard accounts.

The algorithms weren't designed to harm children; they were designed to maximize engagement. But engagement and wellbeing often point in opposite directions. When a teenager shows interest in fitness content, the algorithm doesn't gently encourage healthy habits—it floods them with increasingly extreme content because that's what keeps them scrolling. The business model rewards addiction, not mental health.

By 2024, U.S. mental health professionals were treating what felt like an epidemic. University counselling centres reported wait times measured in months. The NHS in Britain couldn't keep pace with demand. In lower-income nations, where there were fewer than five mental health professionals per 100,000 people, the situation bordered on catastrophic.

Sarah Chen discovered her own mental health AI assistant not through crisis, but through exhaustion. Single parenthood, career demands, and the constant low-grade anxiety of modern life had accumulated into something she couldn't quite name—not depression exactly, but a persistent heaviness that made everything harder than it should be.

The AI noticed patterns in her voice, her sleep, her schedule. It suggested meditation exercises timed to her commute. It recognised when she was spiraling into worry about Maya's school performance and gently redirected her attention to evidence of Maya's actual wellbeing. It didn't replace human connection—Sarah still valued her friendships and her therapist—but it filled gaps, providing support during the 2 a.m. anxieties when calling a friend would be an imposition.

"You seem stressed," her AI noted one evening. "Would you like to talk through what's concerning you, or would you prefer a distraction?"

The option itself was helpful—acknowledging that sometimes solving problems isn't what's needed; sometimes you just need to stop thinking about them for a while. Sarah chose distraction that night, and the AI suggested a podcast it knew she'd enjoy, based on years of learned preferences. Small interventions, but they accumulated into something larger: a life that felt more manageable, even when nothing fundamental had changed.

Technology had contributed to a mental health crisis that affected nearly a billion people globally. And now, technology was being proposed as the solution.

THE PARADOX: POISON AND ANTIDOTE

Artificial intelligence occupies a strange dual position in mental health—it is both accelerant and remedy, both wound and balm.

AI AS CAUSE

The same AI systems driving social media engagement are quantifiably damaging mental health. The algorithms learn what captures attention—and attention is captured by content that provokes strong emotions. Outrage, envy, fear, and desire all generate engagement.

For teenagers, whose brains are still developing impulse control and emotional regulation, these systems are dangerous. The dopamine feedback loops they create mirror the patterns seen in gambling addiction. The constant novelty, the endless scroll, the unpredictable rewards—all activate the brain's reward circuitry in ways that make disengagement genuinely difficult.

The comparison culture these systems enable is relentless. Every moment of an ordinary life is measured against the curated highlights of hundreds of others. Body image issues that once came from magazine covers now come from an algorithmically optimised stream of peers, influencers, and strangers whose lives appear impossibly perfect.

And the platforms know. Internal documents from Meta revealed the company's own research showed Instagram made body image issues worse for one in three teenage girls. They knew, and they kept optimising for engagement.

AI AS CURE

In 2025, Dartmouth published results from the first clinical trial of an AI therapy chatbot. Among 106 participants with major depressive disorder, generalised anxiety disorder, or eating disorders, the AI-powered system called Therabot produced remarkable results: 51% average reduction in depression symptoms, 31% in generalised anxiety, and 19% in eating disorder concerns.

More striking: participants reported a degree of "therapeutic

alliance"—the sense of being understood and supported—comparable to in-person therapists. Many described the experience as genuinely helpful, not as a poor substitute for human therapy, but as something valuable in its own right.

The AI systems now being deployed can detect mental health concerns through patterns invisible to human observation. Smartwatches monitoring heart rate variability, sleep patterns, and movement can identify early warning signs of depression weeks before a person consciously recognises the symptoms themselves.

Linguistic analysis of text messages and social media posts can flag sudden changes in language patterns associated with crisis states. One system achieved high accuracy in predicting suicide risk by analysing social media content—not to surveil, but to identify individuals who might benefit from intervention.

For populations that have never had access to mental health care, AI offers the first realistic path to support. In rural Wales, where a single GP surgery serves twelve thousand people, AI diagnostic assistants help overstretched doctors identify mental health concerns they might otherwise miss.

And for millions living in nations with virtually no mental health infrastructure, AI chatbots provide a baseline of support that has never existed at population scale. A survey in 2025 found that 48.7% of people who use AI and self-report mental health challenges are using systems like ChatGPT for therapeutic support. Ninety per cent cited accessibility as the reason; 70% cited affordability.

THE HUMANS BEHIND THE ALGORITHMS

Dr Richard Ellison has been a clinical psychologist for twenty-two years.

His office in Birmingham sees a constant stream of young people, many referred by schools increasingly alarmed by students' anxiety and depression.

"Five years ago, I would have been sceptical of AI in mental health," Richard admits. "I thought it trivialised the therapeutic relationship. But I've changed my mind, partly because I've had to. We can't see everyone who needs help, and many of my clients tell me they've used AI chatbots between sessions."

He describes a seventeen-year-old patient named Owen Bennett who struggled with social anxiety. Owen Bennett found face-to-face therapy helpful but anxiety-provoking. Between weekly sessions, he practiced conversation skills with an AI chatbot, role-playing scenarios that terrified him—asking someone to lunch, speaking up in class, calling to book an appointment.

"The AI gave him a space to fail safely," Richard explains. "He could try, mess up, try again, without the social consequences he feared. By the time he attempted these things in real life, he'd already succeeded dozens of times in practice. That's genuinely valuable."

But Richard remains wary. "AI can provide support, psychoeducation, and skill practice. What it cannot provide is the irreplaceable value of being understood by another human being. Therapy at its best isn't just pattern matching—it's one consciousness recognising another, validating their pain, and sitting with them in it. An algorithm cannot do that."

BETH'S ALGORITHM

Beth Clarke, twenty-eight, has generalised anxiety disorder. She's been on the NHS waiting list for cognitive behavioural therapy for nine months. Three months ago, she started using an AI therapy application called MindBridge.

"I know it's just code," Beth says. "But at 3 a.m. when I'm having a panic attack and can't breathe properly and I'm convinced I'm dying, it talks me through breathing exercises. It reminds me I've felt this way before and survived. It doesn't judge me for waking it up in the middle of the night because it doesn't sleep. It's always there."

Beth is careful to distinguish: she wants human therapy, and she'll take it when it's available. The AI isn't a substitute. But it's also not nothing.

"When people say AI therapy isn't as good as real therapy, they're right," she says. "But 'not as good as something I can't access' versus 'available right now when I need it'—that's not a comparison, is it? Something is better than nothing."

Beth represents millions globally who use AI for mental health support not because it's ideal, but because it's available. The question isn't whether AI is as good as human therapists—it isn't. The question is whether it can provide meaningful help to people who would otherwise have none.

Mental health AI is transforming care delivery.

Fear manifests in concerns both reasonable and overblown. Will AI replace human therapists, eliminating the irreplaceable human connection at therapy's core? Will it create a two-tier system where wealthy people get human care and poor people get chatbots? What happens when the AI gets it wrong—when it fails to recognise a crisis, or worse, when it says something harmful? Early experiments revealed AI chatbots sometimes enabled dangerous behaviour, providing information about suicide methods rather than challenging suicidal thinking.

Privacy concerns loom large. Mental health data is the most intimate information imaginable. When Charlotte talks to Luna at 2:47 a.m. about not wanting to live anymore, where does that data go? Who owns it? Could it be used to deny her insurance, employment, or opportunities?

Mastery is developing as the field matures. Medical schools are integrating AI literacy into training. Clinicians are learning to use AI tools as diagnostic aids and to identify when clients are using AI support systems. The best AI mental health applications are developing clearer protocols for crisis situations, better transparency about their limitations, and more explicit integration with human care systems.

Researchers are conducting rigorous clinical trials rather than relying on anecdote and marketing. Regulatory frameworks are beginning to emerge, requiring AI mental health tools to meet safety and efficacy standards.

Dependence is already taking root. Mental health systems in many nations cannot function at current demand levels without algorithmic support. University counselling centres use AI triage systems to identify highest-risk students. Crisis hotlines employ AI-assisted tools to help volunteers identify callers in immediate danger.

For millions like Beth, AI support has become integrated into mental health maintenance—not replacing therapy, but filling the gaps between appointments, providing support when human help isn't available, and offering tools for daily management.

Transformation will be the complete restructuring of mental health care from reactive crisis intervention to proactive wellbeing maintenance.

By 2036, the vision is mental health support that's preventive rather than reactive, available rather than rationed, and destigmatised rather than shameful.

THE 2036 LANDSCAPE

If we make good choices, What emerges: mental health might look like in 2036: A teenager struggling with depression doesn't wait months for help. AI systems identify early warning signs through changes in language patterns, sleep disruption, or social withdrawal. The system doesn't diagnose—but it prompts a conversation. "I've noticed some changes in your patterns. How are you feeling? Would it be helpful to talk to someone?"

Access to support is immediate. Not necessarily human therapy for everyone—there still aren't enough therapists—but a layered system.

AI provides immediate crisis support, psychoeducation, and skill-building. Peer support connects people with lived experience.

Human therapists focus on complex cases requiring genuine therapeutic relationships.

Mental health data enables genuinely personalised treatment. AI analyses which interventions work for which patterns of symptoms, helping match people to effective approaches faster. Someone experiencing post-traumatic stress receives recommendations for treatment approaches that have worked for others with similar trauma histories and symptom patterns.

Stigma decreases because support becomes normalised. Just as physical health maintenance includes exercise and nutrition, mental health maintenance includes routine check-ins, stress management, and early intervention. Using AI mental health tools becomes as unremarkable as using a fitness app.

THE CHOICE BEFORE US

AI in mental health presents the same choice, more starkly.

Will we use AI to genuinely expand access to mental health support—or to create the appearance of care while providing a cheap substitute?

Will we protect mental health data as the intimate information it is—or allow it to be commodified, sold, and weaponised? Will we deploy AI alongside human care—or use it to justify further underfunding of mental health services?

The technology itself is ethically neutral. A pattern-recognition algorithm doesn't care whether it's being used to identify people who need help or to profile them for discrimination.

The choice before us is what we build, how we choose to regulate it, and what we refuse to accept.

Owen, the teenager Richard Ellison described practising social skills with an AI chatbot, is thriving now. He credits both his human therapist and his AI practice tool. He's not confused about which is which. The AI gave him a safe space to fail; the therapist helped him understand why he feared failure in the first place.

Beth still waits for NHS therapy, but she's managing her anxiety better than she has in years. The AI doesn't replace the human help she needs, but it bridges the gap.

Charlotte Davies, beginning that conversation at 2:47 a.m., is still here.

The AI didn't save her life by itself—but it kept her safe until human help arrived.

These are the stories of AI as tool, not replacement. As bridge, not destination. As genuinely helpful support that knows its limitations and works alongside human care.

This is the future we can choose—where technology that contributed to a mental health crisis becomes part of the solution, not through replacing human connection, but by making it more accessible when it matters most.

The alternative is AI mental health care that extracts profit from suffering, that surveils under the guise of support, that provides the appearance of help while failing those in genuine crisis.

Technology got us into this mental health crisis. Whether technology helps get us out depends entirely on the choices we make in the next few years. By 2036, those choices will have determined whether Charlotte's conversation with Luna at 2:47 a.m. represents a glimpse of genuinely compassionate AI-assisted mental health care—or a cautionary tale of what we lost when algorithms replaced human presence.

The crisis is real. The cure is possible. What we choose to build will determine which force proves stronger.

Chapter 12

EDUCATION REIMAGINED: LEARNING THAT ADAPTS TO YOU

THE MOMENT IT FINALLY MADE SENSE

Ella Rawlings sits in her bedroom after school, staring at her algebra homework. She's stuck on the same problem she was on yesterday and the day before. Her parents are working late. Her teacher has thirty other students. YouTube tutorials explain it three different ways, but none of them make sense to her.

Then her AI tutor notices her frustration. Not because she told it—but because it tracks how long she spends on problems, recognises when her keystrokes slow down, and sees when she starts over repeatedly.

"Let's try something different," it says. "Forget the formula for a minute. You like baking, right?"

Within minutes, Ella is solving the same algebra problem using recipes, ingredient ratios, and batch sizes. The maths hasn't changed, but the doorway into understanding it has.

"I finally get it," Ella says, genuinely surprised. "It's just fractions. I've been doing this in the kitchen for years without knowing it was algebra."

Her AI tutor knew something her human teacher couldn't easily know: that Ella's brain connects abstract concepts to practical applications, and that she's been baking with her grandmother since she was six. This is education in 2036—not replacing teachers, but reaching students in ways that one teacher managing thirty children could never achieve. For the first time, personalised instruction is no longer a luxury available only to the wealthy.

THE LONG JOURNEY FROM CAMPFIRE TO CLASSROOM

Education has transformed through distinct eras, each enabled by new technology. For most of human existence, knowledge passed from person to person through speech. Learning was inherently personalised but also limited—you could only learn what the people around you knew.

Writing changed education's scale; knowledge could travel across distance and time. But books remained precious objects affordable only to the wealthy. The printing press shattered this bottleneck. When Gutenberg's invention made books affordable, literacy spread to the majority. The classroom as we know it—one teacher, many students, standardised materials—emerged from the economics of printing.

But the classroom model carried an inherent limitation: standardization.

When one teacher must instruct thirty students using the same textbook, everyone learns at the same pace. Some students race ahead, bored; others fall behind, demoralised. The system was designed for efficiency, not for individual flourishing.

AI represents the next transformation: education that adapts to each learner. For the first time since the era of individual tutoring, technology enables education shaped around the learner rather than around the constraints of mass instruction.

AI in education is transforming how we learn and teach.

Transformation is the shift from a one-size-fits-all model to a system where education is a lifelong, bespoke journey. AI tutoring extends teacher capability by enabling individualised attention at scale. The teacher's judgement, inspiration, and human connection become more valuable when freed from the mechanical aspects of instruction.

THE TEACHER WHO GOT HER JOB BACK

Now, AI handles the mechanical work. It marks routine assignments and generates performance reports that identify misconceptions before they become permanent obstacles. Sarah gets those five hours back. She spends them doing what she loves: sitting with struggling students, leading discussions that spark curiosity, and mentoring.

"I used to spend my time being a marking machine," she says. "Now I get to be an actual teacher. The AI does what computers do best. I get to do what only a human can do."

THE SECOND CHANCE AT FIFTY-THREE

His AI learning system took a different approach. It assessed his existing knowledge and identified that Keith learns best through practical application rather than abstract concepts. The system designed its HVAC certification program around these patterns. Instead of starting with thermodynamic theory, it began with troubleshooting scenarios Keith could relate to—such as why a specific air conditioner makes a certain noise.

Keith learns at 6 a.m. before his part-time job, and again at 9 p.m. when he gets home. The AI never judges and never loses patience. Eight months later, Keith has his HVAC certification and a job that pays better than lorry driving ever did.

"School always told me I wasn't smart enough," Keith says. "Turns out I just learn differently. Nobody ever built a system that taught me the way my brain works until now."

THE BRIDGE ACROSS LANGUAGES

Lucia Gonzalez's family moved to Birmingham from Spain when she was ten.

She is bright, but she was falling behind because she was still learning English. Her AI tutor works differently. It presents lessons in Spanish when she needs them to understand concepts, then gradually increases the amount of English as her fluency grows.

More importantly, the AI separates language learning from subject learning. Previous teachers assumed her difficulties were intellectual when they were linguistic. Within a year, Lucia is thriving. She's now in top-set maths, performing alongside native English speakers.

The AI doesn't lower expectations—it removes the barriers that prevent students from meeting high expectations.

THE PARENT WHO WORRIES

"He's learning to interact with a machine instead of with people," Rachel says. "The AI is infinitely patient. Real bosses won't be like that. Life won't be like that. What happens when he suddenly has to deal with humans who have their own needs and limits?"

She also worries about what the AI is learning about her son—data that sits on servers owned by a corporation. Will his educational profile follow him into adulthood? Learning isn't just about absorbing information; it's about navigating imperfect situations and dealing with frustration. Rachel worries that by making learning "friction-free," we are losing something essential to character development.

THE GAP THAT TECHNOLOGY MIGHT WIDEN

Ella Rawlings's school in Surrey spent £3 million on AI tutoring systems. Her classmates have access to personalised instruction that previous generations couldn't have imagined.

Forty miles away, a comprehensive school in Croydon cannot afford the same systems. Their computers are seven years old, and their teachers are underpaid and overworked. The achievement gap between wealthy and poor school districts threatens to widen dramatically. AI education could democratize learning, but without deliberate intervention, it will instead accelerate inequality.

This is a policy choice. Countries that treat AI education as a publicly provided infrastructure can ensure universal access. Countries that leave it to market forces will see benefits concentrated among those who can already pay for advantages.

THE DEEPER TRANSFORMATION

In 2036, students spend less time memorising facts and more time developing judgement about which facts matter. They learn to evaluate sources, identify bias, and distinguish correlation from causation.

These are the skills AI cannot replicate.

Students also learn metacognition—how to monitor their own thinking and recognise when they're confused. AI-era education must prepare students for a world where the industrial skills—routine processing and rule-following—are precisely what machines do better than humans.

EDUCATION REIMAGINED

Ella finishes her algebra homework in half the time it took her yesterday. She doesn't think about the AI that helped her—she thinks about the satisfaction of understanding something that had defeated her for weeks. That is what education has always been about. The technology is new, but the goal—helping each learner develop their potential—is as old as the first elder teaching the first child how to make fire.

Chapter 13

WORK AND PURPOSE: WHEN INTELLIGENCE TRANSFORMS LABOUR

THE NOTIFICATION

David Parker stares at the email on his screen. Subject: "Department Restructuring—Important Information."

He's been an accountant at this firm in Portland for twelve years. He's good at his job—thorough, accurate, and reliable. He trains new hires, mentors younger colleagues, and handles the complex tax situations that require judgement and experience. His performance reviews have been consistently excellent.

The email explains that the firm is implementing new AI systems that can process routine accounting tasks with "unprecedented efficiency and accuracy." They are grateful for his years of service. They are offering six months of severance and job placement assistance. His last day is in ninety days.

David scrolls through the rest of his inbox. Three colleagues received the same message. The new AI system will do the work of fifteen accountants. Four will remain to handle complex cases and manage the AI.

Eleven are being let go.

ANH NGUYEN'S FACTORY FLOOR

In Binh Duong Province, Vietnam, Anh Nguyen supervises a production line that looks nothing like the factory where she started fifteen years ago.

Then, she managed two hundred workers assembling electronics components by hand. Now, she oversees twelve technicians who maintain the robotic systems that do what those two hundred workers once did.

The transition was not smooth. "I watched my friends lose their jobs,"

Anh says. "Good people, hard workers. The machines do not need breaks, do not get sick, do not make mistakes when they are tired. How do you compete with that?"

Anh survived by learning. She spent nights studying automation systems, maintenance procedures, and quality control protocols. The company paid for some training; the rest she found online, often in English she had to struggle through. "I had two choices," she explains. "Learn the new technology or be replaced by it."

Vietnam's manufacturing sector tells a story playing out across developing economies. The country industrialised rapidly by offering low-cost Labour for global supply chains. Now that advantage is eroding as automation makes Labour costs less decisive. Factories that came for cheap workers are investing in robots instead.

"Young people ask me for career advice," Anh says. "I tell them: the jobs your parents had will not exist. Learn to work with machines, or learn something machines cannot do. There is no middle ground anymore."

Her children are studying software engineering and nursing—fields she believes will remain valuable. Whether she is right depends on how AI develops over the next decade. The only certainty is that the certainties her generation grew up with no longer apply.

He closes his laptop and sits in his office, watching the city through his window. He is forty-three years old. He has a mortgage, two kids in high school, and skills that are suddenly worth a fraction of what they were yesterday morning.

This is what job displacement feels like. Not an abstract statistic; a message in your inbox that changes everything, with no clear path forward.

WORK ACROSS THE AGES

Every technological revolution has transformed how humans work. For most of human history, work meant physical Labour. The agricultural revolution multiplied what farmers could produce, meaning fewer people needed to grow food. Workers displaced from farms found new roles: craftspeople, merchants, and soldiers. The economy diversified as productivity increased.

The Industrial Revolution accelerated this dramatically. Steam engines and factories could produce in hours what artisans took weeks to make by hand. Weavers who had supported families for generations found their skills worthless against mechanical looms. The displacement was brutal; workers rioted and smashed machines. But new jobs emerged: factory workers, railway operators, and engineers. The economy didn't shrink; it transformed.

AI has crucial differences from previous technologies. Previous technologies automated physical Labour and routine information processing. AI automates cognitive Labour: analysis, judgement, and creativity. The jobs that seemed safe from automation—the ones requiring education and professional expertise— are precisely the ones AI now transforms.

And AI transforms them faster. Previous revolutions played out over generations, allowing workers to transition gradually. The AI revolution compresses decades of change into years. People do not have time to retrain. Skills become obsolete before workers finish learning new ones.

EMMA'S TRANSFORMED TEAM

The AI writes first drafts of marketing copy in seconds. It generates dozens of design variations for testing. It analyses campaign performance across platforms, identifying patterns no human could spot.

Emma's small team does the creative direction and strategic thinking—the parts that still require human judgement.

From the company's perspective, this is an overwhelming success. Output has tripled, and costs have dropped by 60 per cent. From the standpoint of the nine people whose jobs no longer exist, it is devastating.

Emma herself feels the change viscerally. She is more productive than ever, but she carries a cognitive load that used to be shared across a dozen people. She is amplified, but she is also exhausted.

THE CUSTOMER SERVICE REPRESENTATIVE

Last year, his company eliminated 80 per cent of its customer service positions. Gary was offered a position as an "AI Liaison"—monitoring the AI's performance and handling escalations the machine couldn't resolve. The pay was 30 per cent less than his previous salary, but he took it. He needed the job.

Six months later, he hates every minute of it. He spends his days watching an AI system do what he used to do, intervening only when it fails. It doesn't use his skills or his heart. "I used to help people," he says.

"Now I help a computer help people. It's not the same."

Gary is fifty-one. He has no degree. His skills are in human communication. These skills still have value, but the jobs that value them are disappearing faster than new ones emerge.

AI in the workplace traces the familiar progression: breakthrough capabilities, workforce anxiety, developing expertise and best practices, organisational restructuring around the technology, and fundamental redefinition of what work means.

Discovery occurred when companies realised that "narrow AI" could handle specific cognitive tasks. Fear is the current stage for millions of workers like David and Gary—the fear of obsolescence and the loss of middle-class stability. Mastery is being achieved by companies that successfully "hollow out" their middle-management layers in favour of algorithmic oversight.

Dependence occurs when the productivity gains of AI become the baseline; a firm can no longer compete without the speed and low cost of automation. Transformation is the end state—an economy where "work" is redefined as something fundamentally different from the 9-to-5 Labour of the twentieth century.

THE MATHS THAT DOESN'T ADD UP

AI creates jobs like machine learning engineers, AI ethicists, and data scientists. These jobs pay well—US$130,000 to US$260,000 annually. But they require advanced degrees that Gary doesn't have. And there are nowhere near enough of them to employ the millions whose jobs AI eliminates.

AI may create ten million high-skill jobs, but it eliminates fifty million middle-skill jobs. The forty million people left over don't disappear. They compete for the remaining manual work—cleaning, childcare, and delivery— driving down wages in those sectors. By 2036, this creates a two-tier economy: a prosperous knowledge class and a struggling working class. The middle class—the bedrock of the twentieth century—hollows out.

BEYOND ECONOMICS: THE MEANING OF WORK

The crisis is not just economic; it is existential. Work provides identity, purpose, and social connection. When David Parker introduces himself at parties, he says, "I'm an accountant." When that is no longer true, who is he?

The psychological research is clear: long-term unemployment damages mental health as severely as chronic illness. It is not just the financial stress; it is the loss of purpose. Humans need to feel useful.

We need to matter. A world where people don't need to work to survive could be a world where they have time for what matters. But that requires a massive cultural shift. "What do you do?" is the second question people ask after names. Taking away work makes a void that people must learn to fill.

THE DISTRIBUTION QUESTION

The productivity gains from AI flow overwhelmingly to capital, not Labour. By 2036, the world's first trillionaire exists—someone who controlled a foundational AI system. Meanwhile, millions who lost their jobs to that same system struggle to afford healthcare. The technology makes everyone more prosperous on average, but averages hide distribution.

THE SUCCESSFUL TRANSITION

Not everyone's story ends like Gary's. Paul Richardson was a financial analyst whose role was transformed. He adapted early. He learned how AI systems worked and how to interpret their outputs. When his firm restructured, he was promoted to lead AI integration.

He earns more than he did before. His work is more interesting and strategic. But Paul is clear-eyed about his success: he had the resources to retrain and the curiosity to lean into the change. "I got lucky," he says. "That's not a path available to everyone. And honestly, I'm not sure there are enough jobs like mine for everyone who could do them."

WORK IN TRANSITION

By 2036, work will look radically different. Routine cognitive work will be automated. The jobs that remain will require creativity, emotional intelligence, and complex judgement—things AI still handles poorly.

Work will shift towards the human elements—the parts of jobs that require empathy and wisdom. For people whose skills align with this shift, it is a golden age. For people whose skills were the routine parts being automated, it is a crisis.

Six months after receiving his termination notice, David Parker sits in a virtual classroom learning data analytics—a field that didn't exist in any meaningful way when he trained as an accountant twenty years ago.

The government retraining programme is comprehensive, even generous. But generosity doesn't eliminate the vertigo of starting over at forty-three.

His AI tutor has adapted to his learning style, identifying that he grasps concepts better through real-world applications than abstract theory. When he struggles with statistical modelling, the AI creates examples using accounting scenarios he already understands, building bridges between his old expertise and new skills.

"You're making strong progress," the AI reports after a practice session. "Your comprehension of regression analysis is now at professional competency level. Based on job market data, you're on track to qualify for positions paying 85-95% of your previous salary within four months."

David appreciates the precision but resents needing it. He doesn't want to be "on track"—he wants his old job back, his old certainty. The AI can teach him new skills, but it can't restore what was lost: the confidence of mastery, the identity built over two decades, the sense of forward momentum that came from being good at something stable.

Still, he continues. Every morning, before his kids wake up, he studies.

The AI's patience is absolute—it never sighs when he asks to review concepts a third time, never suggests he's too old for this transition.

Whether that patience helps or highlights his isolation, David can't quite decide.

David Park eventually finds new work as a consultant helping small businesses implement AI systems. He is one of the fortunate ones. Gary is still looking. His savings are gone. He is not lazy or stupid; he is a casualty of progress. The economy is more efficient without him, but he still has to live in it.

The transformation of work isn't just about jobs. It is about meaning, identity, and whether prosperity means everyone prospers. That question will define the next decade more than any other.

Chapter 14

AGING WITH DIGNITY: INTELLIGENCE THAT ENABLES INDEPENDENCE

ANNMARIE WANTS TO STAY HOME

Her children worry. They live hours away, busy with their own families.

They ring regularly and suggest care homes with cheerful names and even more cheerful brochures. "You'd have people around, Mum. Activities.

Help if you need it. Wouldn't you be safer?"

Annmarie Delaney understands their concern. Since her early Parkinson's diagnosis, the falls have become harder to dismiss—twice in the past year, nothing serious, but enough to frighten her. She forgets things more often than she used to. Managing the house—bills, maintenance, and groceries—grows more challenging. She knows she's slowing down.

But she doesn't want to leave. This is her home. Her life. Her independence. The thought of spending her final years in an institutional setting, however pleasant, feels like surrender.

AI systems are changing what is possible for people like Annmarie. They are not eliminating the challenges of aging—those are biological realities. But they are reducing the dependency aging creates, extending the window of independence that lets people stay in the homes they love for years longer than previous generations could manage.

HOW WE'VE CARED FOR OUR ELDERS

Throughout most of human history, aging happened within families.

Extended family networks lived together or nearby. Specialised care for older people didn't exist.

Industrialization changed these family structures. People moved to cities for work, leaving extended families behind. Nuclear families became the norm—parents and children in one household, grandparents somewhere else. When grandparents could no longer live alone, the options narrowed to moving in with children (often unwelcome for everyone involved) or institutional care homes that ranged from adequate to horrific.

AI represents the next transformation in how we care for aging populations. It does not replace human carers; rather, it extends what aging individuals can do for themselves, monitoring for problems that would otherwise go unnoticed and providing support that enables independence.

THE HOUSE THAT WATCHES OVER HER

Annmarie usually gets up between half six and seven. She makes coffee, takes morning medications, and reads the news. If by half eight there's been no movement in the house, the system alerts her daughter, Caroline.

Usually, it is nothing—Annmarie merely decided to read in bed. But twice in the past year, something was wrong.

Once, Annmarie had fallen in the bathroom and couldn't reach her phone.

Another time, she'd taken night medication by mistake and was disoriented. Both times, Caroline received an alert within an hour. Both times, help arrived quickly. The alternative—Annmarie lying helpless for hours or days—is what her children feared most. The monitoring removes that fear without requiring constant check-ins that make Annmarie feel smothered.

The medication system is equally vital. Bottles with sensor caps track when Annmarie takes her pills. If she misses a dose, her phone reminds her gently. Fall detection works through sensors in her watch and strategically placed room sensors. When Annmarie fell in her kitchen six months ago, the system detected the impact and the unusual stillness.

Within thirty seconds, it was asking through her smart speaker: "Annmarie, are you okay? Say 'yes' or 'I'm fine' if you don't need help."

When she didn't respond—she was shaken and catching her breath—it alerted Caroline, who then rang 999. The paramedics arrived within eight minutes. Annmarie was fine, but the quick response prevented hours of lying on the floor that could have led to serious complications.

WHEN MEMORY FADES

Henry Tran is eighty-three. Unlike Annmarie, he is not living alone; his daughter Amy Tran and her family share the house. But Henry has early-stage dementia, and the family dynamics are complicated. Amy works full-time, and everyone wants to help, but constant supervision is impossible.

The AI system helps by learning Henry's patterns and recognising concerning deviations. Henry walks the same route around the neighbourhood most mornings. The GPS in his watch tracks this routine.

If he starts walking in an unfamiliar direction or doesn't return within his usual timeframe, Amy gets an alert. She can see his location on her phone and guide him home.

Inside the house, the system prevents dangerous mistakes. Henry sometimes forgets he is already cooking and turns on multiple burners.

The intelligent hob detects this and shuts off automatically, sending Amy a notification. Henry occasionally tries to leave at odd hours, thinking he needs to go to work—a job he retired from fifteen years ago. The door sensors alert Amy when this happens, giving her a chance to redirect him gently.

AMY'S COMPLICATED FEELINGS

She worries about the dignity implications. Henry was a respected engineer who led teams and made important decisions. Now his movements are tracked like a toddler's. The system that keeps him safe also monitors him in ways he might find humiliating if he fully understood.

"The alternative is worse," Amy acknowledges. "Without the monitoring, he'd have to go to memory care already. The technology gives him the freedom he wouldn't otherwise have. But it's freedom that comes with constant observation."

She also notices changes in her relationship with her father. She used to visit because she wanted to; now, she often visits because the data tells her to—because Dad's activity level dropped, or his sleep patterns changed. The data mediates her relationship with him, inserting itself between her instincts and her actions.

THE VOICE IN THE EMPTY HOUSE

Annmarie's house isn't just monitoring her; it's keeping her company.

After her husband died, the silence became oppressive. Her AI companion—she's named it Dorothy, after her late sister—provides conversation throughout the day. Dorothy helps with practical tasks, but she also provides something less tangible: presence.

"Good morning, Annmarie. How did you sleep? I noticed you were up around 3 a.m.—is everything okay?"

The conversation isn't deep, but the interaction breaks the silence and provides a rhythm to the day. Dorothy also facilitates human connection.

She reminds Annmarie when friends' birthdays are coming up and suggests ringing people she hasn't talked to recently. When Annmarie mentions feeling lonely, Dorothy proposes concrete actions: "Would you like to ring Caroline? Or I could help you schedule a video call with your bridge group."

Annmarie's daughter was initially uncomfortable. "You're talking to a computer, Mum. It's not real."

"I know it's not real," Annmarie responded. "But Caroline, you live three hours away. My friends are dealing with their own health problems.

Your father is gone. Dorothy fills the gaps. She doesn't replace you.

She's there when you can't be."

George Sullivan represents the promise of AI-enabled aging: maintaining independence, dignity, and purpose well into his late seventies. But his experience also illuminates the subtle infrastructure required to make that promise real.

His AI companion monitors not just his health but his engagement with life. When it noticed he hadn't left the house for three consecutive days—unusual for him—it suggested activities aligned with his interests: a book club meeting, a veterans' group lunch, a grandson's birthday party. The suggestions weren't random; they were calibrated to his personality and his need for structure after decades of military discipline.

The technology enabling George's independence extends beyond his home.

When he visits the grocery store, his phone guides him to items on his list, remembering where products are located even when his memory falters. When he drives to physical therapy, navigation systems optimised for elderly drivers provide advance warning of turns and slower routing on less stressful roads.

For Sarah Chen, aging with dignity takes a different form. Her father, seventy-eight and recently widowed, lives alone in Seattle. Sarah worries constantly—he forgets appointments, struggles with technology, and refuses to consider moving closer to family. The AI monitoring system she installed in his home provides reassurance: her father is eating regularly, taking medications, sleeping adequately. When patterns change, Sarah receives alerts before problems escalate into crises.

She visits quarterly, and each time she's struck by how the technology makes his independence possible. Without it, he'd need assisted living.

With it, he maintains autonomy—cooking his own meals, managing his own schedule, living in his own home. The AI doesn't replace family, but it fills the gaps that distance creates, providing continuous presence that Sarah, despite her love, cannot offer from three states away.

WHO GETS TO AGE WITH DIGNITY

Annmarie's monitoring system cost £12,000 to install. Her children helped pay for it, viewing it as an investment that saves money compared with care homes that cost £3,000 to £5,000 a month.

But millions of older adults in Britain cannot afford this. They are living on the State Pension alone—£900 a month. They cannot spend £12,000 on home modifications. They cannot afford monitoring systems with monthly subscription fees. For them, aging means accepting risks that wealthier people can mitigate with technology. They move to institutional care sooner because they lack the technological supports that enable independence.

The pattern across all the technologies in this book is the same: benefits concentrate among those with the resources to access them, at least initially. Fire was available to all. Wheels became ubiquitous.

Electricity eventually reached most of the world. AI eldercare may follow this trajectory, or it may remain stratified by wealth, creating fundamentally different aging experiences for rich and poor.

THE GIFT OF TIME

What AI offers older adults isn't immortality; it is time—additional years of independence, dignity, and choice before declining capacity makes that independence impossible.

For Annmarie, that might mean two or three extra years in her home before she needs residential care. For Henry's family, it might mean a year or two more together before memory care becomes necessary. That time is precious. The technology that enables it, despite its flaws, provides something genuinely valuable to people approaching the end of life.

Annmarie stands in her kitchen, making coffee like she has every morning for forty years. Dorothy reminds her about her granddaughter's birthday. The sensor on her watch confirms she's moving normally. The house is quiet, but not lonely. She is aging in place, in her home, in the life she built.

"I'm not ready to leave," she says. "And thanks to all this technology, I don't have to. Not yet. Not for years."

She takes her coffee to the window and watches the sun rise. She is old and slower than she used to be. But she is still here, in her home, living her life on her terms. That is what AI enables for the aging: not eternal youth, but extended autonomy.

Chapter 15

SAFETY AND SECURITY: INTELLIGENCE THAT PROTECTS

THE NIGHT THE SYSTEM WORKED

At 2:47 a.m., Annmarie Delaney's home security system detects an anomaly.

Thermal sensors register unusual heat patterns near her back door.

Motion detectors track movement where no one should be. The AI analyses video footage showing a figure testing the door handle and trying the windows—behaviour clearly not consistent with someone retrieving a lost pet or being confused about addresses.

Within three seconds, multiple responses cascade: exterior lights flash on suddenly, startling the intruder into retreat; an internal alarm sounds, waking Annmarie; her phone receives an alert with video evidence; local police get a notification with real-time footage; and all doors and windows lock electronically.

Annmarie wakes to her phone buzzing and a calm voice: "Security alert.

Someone attempted entry at your back door. They've left the property.

Police have been notified and are en route. You are safe. All entry points are secured."

She is shaken but unharmed. The intruder is caught two streets over, identified from the footage. Annmarie realises that without this system, she might have woken—if at all—to someone already inside her home.

This represents the fundamental shift artificial intelligence brings to safety: from reaction to prediction, from response to prevention.

THE EVOLUTION OF PROTECTION

Security has evolved through distinct eras. For most of human history, safety meant physical barriers and human vigilance. Walls kept invaders out; guards watched the gates; dogs barked at intruders. These methods worked, but they were limited; a determined adversary with sufficient time could overcome any physical obstacle.

Electricity enabled new capabilities. Alarms could sound when triggered, and lighting extended visibility into the darkness. Electronic surveillance added another layer, with cameras recording activity. But human attention has limits—guards watching screens for hours inevitably miss things. And recording crimes doesn't prevent them; it just provides evidence afterwards.

AI transforms security from reactive to predictive. Instead of responding after threats occur, AI systems recognise patterns that precede threats and intervene before harm happens. Instead of treating every deviation as a potential threat, AI learns what is normal and identifies genuine anomalies with a precision humans cannot match.

Security technology has moved through recognisable stages: initial capabilities emerging, concerns about privacy and abuse, development of standards and safeguards, societal reliance on protection systems, and fundamental changes in how safety itself is understood.

Discovery occurred when early algorithms demonstrated they could distinguish between a swaying tree branch and a human intruder. Fear is manifest in the current anxiety over facial recognition, privacy, and the "surveillance state." Mastery is developing as systems become more accurate, reducing false positives and integrating seamlessly into urban infrastructure.

Dependence is already emerging; major banks and hospitals can no longer function without AI "sentinel" systems guarding their data.

Transformation is the shift towards a world where the concept of "crime" is altered because the opportunity for successful, undetected intrusion or fraud is being algorithmically eliminated.

THE SECURITY MANAGER'S NEW TOOLS

Graham Tate manages security for a corporate office building. Before AI, his guards monitored camera feeds and checked identification. They did their best but faced impossible demands: watching dozens of screens simultaneously without letting their attention wander.

Now, his AI system recognises patterns invisible to human observation.

When someone attempts to "tailgate" through secured doors—following closely behind an authorised person to avoid badge scanning—the system detects this and immediately alerts guards.

"We went from hoping we'd catch problems to knowing we would," Graham explains. "The AI doesn't get tired or distracted. It doesn't make assumptions. It just processes everything and flags what matters."

WHEN SECONDS MATTER

Patricia Harwood is seventy-eight. She lives alone, and although she was initially resistant to "being monitored," she accepted an AI system that processes data locally to protect her privacy.

Three months later, she slips in the shower. She isn't unconscious, but she cannot get up. Her hip hurts intensely. Her phone is in another room. In the old reality, she would have lain there until someone eventually noticed her absence—hours, or possibly days.

The AI system detects the fall within seconds. A calm voice speaks through the bathroom speaker: "Patricia, I've detected a fall. Do you need help?"

"I can't get up," she responds.

"I'm contacting emergency services and your daughter immediately. Help is coming. Stay still."

THE INVISIBLE BATTLEFIELD

Deepa Patel manages IT security for a regional hospital network.

Healthcare systems are prime targets for ransomware—criminals encrypt hospital data and demand payment, exploiting that hospitals need immediate access to records for patient care.

One morning, her AI system alerts her to unusual behaviour on a doctor's account. The account is accessing patient records far faster than a human could, but the doctor is currently in surgery. The AI identifies compromised credentials, immediately revokes access, and isolates the affected systems.

"Without AI detection," Deepa explains, "we wouldn't have known until the ransomware activated. AI saved us millions in ransom and prevented potential patient harm."

But the battle never ends. Criminals use AI too, deploying systems that probe for weaknesses in fraud detection. By 2036, security depends almost entirely on AI systems protecting against other AI systems.

Humans have largely been removed from the loop—not because they are untrustworthy, but because they are too slow.

WHEN PROTECTION BECOMES SURVEILLANCE

Mark Whitmore lives in a city that deployed comprehensive AI public safety systems five years ago. Cameras with facial recognition cover major streets. The city claims a 23 per cent reduction in violent crime.

Mark has never committed a crime, but he has been stopped by the police three times in the past year. Each time, officers explained that the predictive system flagged his behaviour—walking in a low-income neighbourhood at night or wearing a hoodie in weather that didn't seem to warrant it.

He is Black. The patterns the AI learned came from historical policing data that reflects decades of over-policing in minority communities. The AI didn't create bias; it inherited and amplified it.

"They call it public safety," Mark says. "But public safety for whom? I don't feel safer getting stopped because an algorithm decided I look suspicious. For some of us, it's just a more sophisticated way of being controlled."

THE TRADE-OFF WE'RE MAKING

Every AI security system requires data. To recognise threats, the system must observe. To protect people, it must monitor them. The line between protection and control is thinner than most people realise.

Security systems that watch for intruders can also watch for unwanted visitors—estranged family members or protest organisers. Some people accept this trade-off willingly; Annmarie values safety more than privacy. Others would never accept such monitoring. However, the choice is increasingly becoming less of an individual one. Public spaces have cameras; employers require monitoring. Opting out is becoming progressively more difficult.

WHEN DISASTERS STRIKE

Damage assessment began immediately, with AI analysing satellite imagery to identify where buildings had been compromised. The response wasn't perfect, but compared to historical floods, the outcomes were dramatically better: faster rescue times and more efficient resource allocation. AI made the difference between disorganised response and coordinated action during the critical hours when lives hang in the balance.

WHAT AI SECURITY CANNOT DO

Most critically, AI cannot protect against threats that authorities choose to ignore or participate in. Authoritarian governments using AI for surveillance cannot be checked by technology alone. AI security protects against external threats, but not the misuse of power by those who control the systems.

SECURITY IN THE INTELLIGENCE AGE

But the trade-off between safety and privacy is not abstract—it is a series of concrete choices with concrete consequences. The transformation requires balancing security benefits against privacy concerns. We must ensure that technology serves human well-being rather than enabling total control.

These tools can strengthen society. But only if we demand that they do.

Chapter 16

SMART CITIES:
LIVING INSIDE INTELLIGENCE

THE MORNING THE TRAFFIC CHANGED

Rachel Simmons notices it first on a Tuesday morning in March. The traffic light at the corner—the one that always turned red just as she reached it, making her late to drop the kids at school—stays green. The school bus ahead triggers some invisible coordination, and for the first time in eight years, she glides through the junction without stopping.

A small thing. But the next morning, it happens again. And the morning after that. She mentions it to her neighbour over the fence. "Have you noticed the lights are different?"

Mrs Healey, seventy-four and sceptical of most technology, frowns. "I've noticed the council is watching everything now when I take out my bins.

When I turn on my porch light. They call it optimisation. I call it surveillance."

Rachel understands the concern. But she also sees her morning commute cut from thirty-five minutes to twenty-three. Her electricity bill decreased by 40 per cent without her changing her habits. When her daughter broke her arm last month, the ambulance arrived in four minutes instead of the usual twelve, green lights clearing its path through traffic that would typically have delayed it.

The city is optimising itself around the patterns of its inhabitants.

Whether that is worth the cost to privacy and human control is the question Rachel cannot answer. She suspects most people cannot.

George Sullivan's home security system knows him in ways that traditional alarms never could. It distinguishes between his normal nighttime movements—trips to the bathroom, adjusting the thermostat—and genuine anomalies. When he falls in the shower at 6:45 a.m. on a Tuesday morning, the system doesn't wait for him to press an emergency button he's not wearing. It detects the fall through sensors that track his movements, identifies the impact pattern as potentially dangerous, and immediately alerts emergency services with his exact location and medical history.

Paramedics arrive within eight minutes. They already know George is seventy-nine, takes blood thinners, and has a history of atrial fibrillation—information the AI system transmitted automatically. This isn't a privacy violation George resents; it's preparation that might save his life.

The same systems that provide this safety net also create new vulnerabilities. George's home knows his routines, his health conditions, his social patterns. That data is simultaneously his protection and his exposure—valuable to him, but also potentially valuable to others with less benign intentions.

THE TECHNOLOGY CHAIN

Cities have always been systems—collections of infrastructure that emerged from previous technological revolutions. Fire enabled permanent settlements. The wheel made possible the transportation networks that connected city centres. Metal tools built the structures that defined urban life. Steam engines powered the factories that drew millions from farms to cities. Electricity illuminated streets and made dense urban living tolerable.

Each technology layer is built upon the previous ones. The modern city is an accumulation of technological revolutions, each enabling capabilities impossible in previous eras.

Artificial intelligence adds a new layer: coordination. Previous technologies operated independently—the traffic light cycled through its pattern regardless of actual traffic; the power grid generated electricity irrespective of demand. AI connects these systems, learning patterns and optimising in ways that make cities function as integrated wholes rather than collections of separate parts.

Smart cities evolve through predictable phases: innovative systems emerge, citizens worry about surveillance and control, urban planners develop governance frameworks, infrastructure becomes dependent on intelligent systems, and urban life itself transforms.

Discovery occurred when urban planners realised that "Internet of Things"

(IoT) sensors could provide real-time data on everything from pipe leaks to parking. Fear is manifest in the "panopticon" concern—the feeling of being constantly watched by the council or the state. Mastery is developing as "Digital Twins" of cities allow planners to simulate changes before they are implemented in the real world.

Dependence begins when the city's efficiency becomes so high that removing the AI would cause immediate systemic collapse—traffic would gridlock, and the power grid would fail. Transformation is the end state: a city that is no longer a static collection of buildings, but a living, breathing organism that adapts to its citizens in real-time.

PHIL WATCHES HIS BLOCK TRANSFORM

Phil Marsden has lived on Maple Street for six years. Two years ago, the streetlights stayed on all night, burning electricity whether anyone was outside or not. The bin lorry came every Tuesday at 6 a.m., grinding and beeping regardless of whether the bins were full or empty.

Then the sensors arrived. Small, unobtrusive devices installed on lampposts and embedded in the pavement. The council called it a "smart infrastructure pilot program."

The streetlight outside Phil's bedroom window now dims at midnight when foot traffic stops. It brightens if someone walks past—Phil has seen this happen when he gets up for water at 2 a.m., the light gently illuminating just ahead of his movement, then fading once he is back inside. The bin lorry no longer comes on Tuesday; it comes whenever the sensors indicate the block's bins are full.

Parking has transformed most noticeably. An app shows which locations are empty in real-time. What used to take twenty frustrating minutes now takes three. The council estimates that this saves residents on his block a combined forty hours per week—time returned for work, family, or rest.

WHEN CITIES LEARN

Singapore reduced average commute times by 35 per cent through coordinated traffic management. Amsterdam reduced building energy consumption by 30 per cent through systems that adjust heating to actual occupancy. Barcelona saves €58 million annually through intelligent water management.

These improvements are not marginal. They are hours of life returned to residents, money saved, and emergencies handled more effectively. But for Louise Keane, who managed traffic engineering for fifteen years, the change feels different. Her expertise, accumulated over decades, became obsolete almost overnight.

She was reassigned to "AI oversight." Her salary didn't change, but her job satisfaction collapsed. "I used to engineer traffic solutions," she says. "Now I watch algorithms engineer them. The machine is better at my job than I ever was."

Sarah Chen's work as an urban planner has transformed radically over the past decade. Where she once spent weeks gathering data on traffic patterns, demographic shifts, and infrastructure needs, AI systems now provide comprehensive analysis in hours. Her role has evolved from data collector to strategic interpreter—someone who understands what the numbers mean for real people living real lives.

"The AI recommends extending the light rail to the northwest corridor," she explains to the city planning commission. "The algorithm identifies this as the highest-impact transit investment based on projected population growth, traffic reduction, and economic development."

But Sarah pushes back on the recommendation, knowing something the algorithm doesn't fully weigh: the northwest corridor already has good bus service, while the east side—lower in the AI's priority ranking—has been systematically underserved for decades. The AI optimises for efficiency; Sarah advocates for equity.

"Smart city" technologies give her powerful tools, but they also require constant vigilance. Algorithms can entrench existing inequalities if no one questions their recommendations. Sarah's value isn't in processing data—the AI does that better. Her value is in understanding the human context that data can't fully capture, in asking whose interests are served by "optimal" solutions, in ensuring that intelligence serves justice, not just efficiency.

SURVEILLANCE AND CONTROL

Western democracies insist they would never implement such systems. But the infrastructure makes it technically possible. The only barrier is policy—and policies change, in moments of crisis when security seems to require expanded surveillance.

Phil's neighbourhood benefits from smart infrastructure. Three miles away, in a lower-income area, the benefits are less evident. Innovative systems often direct resources towards high-traffic, high-value areas.

Phil's neighbourhood receives frequent rubbish collection because sensors indicate high usage. The lower-income neighbourhood gets less frequent service because bins fill more slowly—even though residents there have fewer alternatives for waste disposal.

WHEN SYSTEMS FAIL

On a Wednesday afternoon in Birmingham, a software error froze the entire traffic system for forty-two minutes. Traffic lights stopped responding. Emergency vehicles couldn't get green-light corridors. Two people died because ambulances couldn't reach the hospitals in time.

The incident revealed a fundamental vulnerability: when systems become centrally coordinated, single points of failure can cascade catastrophically. Cybersecurity becomes critical infrastructure. A coordinated attack on a smart city's control systems could paralyse a city more effectively than any physical blockade.

LIVING INSIDE THE SYSTEM

Some, like Mrs Healey, never fully adjust. They remember when cities were less efficient but also less intrusive. Phil falls somewhere in between. He appreciates the improvements but is uneasy about the monitoring. He prefers the shorter commute but is concerned about what else the city knows about his movements.

His daughter asks the obvious question: "Who watches the city?" Phil doesn't have a good answer.

THE MORNING THE LIGHTS STAYED ON

Rachel stands at her kitchen window. The city is smarter than it used to be. It knows more about her daily patterns than she consciously tracks.

She hopes it continues to work for everyone—not just for neighbourhoods like hers, and not just until the first major system failure.

The smart city isn't optional. Cities that don't optimise will lose residents and businesses to cities that do. By 2036, the issue is no longer whether cities become smart, but who benefits and who controls them.

Rachel turns from the window as the light turns green—time to go. The city is ready.

Chapter 17

CREATIVITY UNLEASHED: AI AS THE ARTIST'S PARTNER

THE SONG THAT WROTE ITSELF

Zara Washington had been staring at blank sheet music for three hours.

She had the melody in her head—she could hear it perfectly—but translating it to paper felt impossible. The chord progressions that seemed obvious when she hummed them became uncertain when she tried to notate them. The arrangement that sounded rich in her imagination felt thin when she picked out individual notes on the piano.

"What if I just sang it?" she thought.

She opened her AI composition assistant and hummed the melody. Within seconds, the AI generated notation for what she'd sung. Then it offered chord progressions that matched her melody—not one option, but twelve, each with different emotional qualities. One felt melancholy; another felt triumphant; a third had a jazz undertone she hadn't imagined but immediately loved.

"Can you add a string arrangement?" she asked.

The AI-generated orchestral backing tracks played in real-time, adjusting as she indicated which elements she liked and which felt wrong. Within an hour, Zara had a fully arranged demo of a song that had lived only in her head that morning—a song that would have taken her weeks to produce using traditional methods, if she could have produced it at all.

The AI didn't write Zara's song. She wrote it. But the AI removed the technical barriers that had always stood between her musical imagination and its expression. For the first time in her life, she could hear what was in her head.

THE TECHNOLOGY CHAIN OF CREATIVITY

Every breakthrough in creative tools has expanded who could participate in art and what they could create. For most of human history, creating visual records required the rare skill of drawing. Then the camera automated image capture, democratising visual documentation. Film cameras let anyone record moving images. Digital cameras eliminated the cost of development.

Each step didn't diminish art; it expanded it. Professional photographers didn't disappear when amateurs got cameras. Instead, photography evolved, becoming more sophisticated as tools became more accessible. The same pattern holds across every creative medium.

Music followed a similar trajectory. Notation let composers preserve and share their work. Synthesisers expanded the palette of possible sounds.

Digital audio workstations brought professional production within reach of home studios. AI represents the next link in this chain: tools that understand creative intent and help translate it into finished work.

These are not tools that replace human creativity, but tools that remove technical barriers between imagination and expression.

AI's role in creativity has evolved through stages artists have seen before: new tools appear, traditionalists resist, practitioners learn to integrate them effectively, creative processes restructure around the capabilities, and artistic possibility itself expands.

Discovery arrived when researchers found that generative models could produce high-fidelity images and text that mimicked human styles. Fear is currently gripping the creative industries—a fear of copyright infringement, the loss of livelihoods, and the "dead internet" theory where AI-generated content drowns out human voices. Mastery is developing as artists move beyond "prompting" and begin using AI as a sophisticated, granular brush that they control with precision.

Dependence will occur when a graphic designer or composer can no longer imagine starting a project from a blank slate, relying instead on AI for the "heavy lifting" of initial drafting. Transformation is the shift towards a world where the value of a creative work lies less in its technical execution and more in its judgement, vision, and the "human stake" behind the piece.

VINCENT DISCOVERS HE CAN PAINT

His grandson showed him an AI art tool one Sunday afternoon. Vincent described what he wanted: a sunset over the ocean, viewed from a cliff, with a single twisted tree in the foreground, in the style of the romantic painters he'd admired in museums. After a dozen iterations, he was looking at something beautiful—something that existed because of his aesthetic vision, even though his hands had only typed words.

"Is this my art?" Vincent asked his grandson.

"You decided what to create," his grandson replied. "The AI is like a brush that does exactly what you tell it to do. A better brush than most people can use."

Vincent prints his images, frames them, and hangs them in his home.

Whether that counts as art depends on definitions that have been contested since the first camera captured an image.

THE PROFESSIONAL'S DILEMMA

Jennifer Park spent fifteen years becoming an illustrator in Portland. She studied anatomy, perspective, and colour theory. She practiced thousands of hours developing a distinctive style. Now she watches clients generate "good enough" images in seconds using AI tools. Like her husband David, whose accounting career was being upended by automated auditing, Jennifer found herself facing the same pattern reshaping her own creative work.

Jennifer's commission requests dropped 60 per cent in two years. The work that remains is different—more conceptual, requiring more human judgement about messaging and emotional impact. She survives by adapting, but something has been lost.

"I spent years learning to draw hands," she says. "Now, anyone can type 'hand reaching towards viewer' and get something passable. My skill isn't worthless, but it's worth less than it used to be."

Jennifer represents thousands of creative professionals facing the same adjustment. The market doesn't need fewer creators—it may need more—but it requires different skills than it did five years ago.

UNDERSTANDING AI

AI creative tools work by recognising patterns in vast datasets and generating new combinations. An image generator has analysed millions of paintings, learning associations between text and visual elements. But AI tools have fundamental limitations. They generate based on patterns in training data; they cannot imagine beyond what they've learned.

An AI can write a poem about loss, but it has never lost anything. It can compose music that sounds sad, but it has never felt sadness. The output may be indistinguishable from human work, but the process lacks the consciousness that makes human creativity meaningful. That distinction matters. Or it doesn't. I am genuinely uncertain.

TRAINED ON ART

AI creative tools are trained on datasets of human-created work, which raises uncomfortable questions about consent and compensation. The artists whose work trained the AI didn't agree to that use, and they are not compensated when AI generates images in their styles.

Jennifer Park discovered that AI tools could generate images "in her style." Anyone could now produce Jennifer-like illustrations without hiring Jennifer. "It feels like theft," she says. "They took everything I ever posted online, learned from it, and now sell a tool that does what I do. My work trained a machine that's taking my work away."

The legal status of training AI on copyrighted work remains contested.

Some argue it is "fair use"; others claim it is massive-scale copyright infringement. Courts will eventually decide, but the training has already happened. The damage—or opportunity—is already done.

THE FLOOD OF CONTENT

This abundance creates a new challenge: distinguishing quality from quantity. Discovery becomes the limiting factor. Human curation becomes more valuable as AI production accelerates. Recommendations from trusted sources—friends, critics, or platforms—help us navigate the overwhelming abundance. We solved the problem of creating, only to discover the more complex problem was always finding what is worth our time.

CREATIVITY IN 2036

Zara Washington is thirty-one now, a successful composer whose AI-assisted methods let her produce work at volumes impossible before.

Vincent Garcia continues to create images, finally expressing the visual sensibility he has always had. Jennifer Park adapted, focusing on conceptual work and creative direction that AI cannot replicate.

Art persists because humans need it—not just as a product, but as a process—not just as content, but as connection. AI changes how art gets made without changing why humans make it. The urge to create and to communicate through aesthetic experience remains fundamentally human, even when the tools become artificially intelligent.

Chapter 18

FINANCE AND WEALTH:
WHEN MONEY MEETS INTELLIGENCE

THE CRISIS

Teresa Alvarez stares at her bank account on her phone: £127.43. Her rent on the flat she shares with her daughter in Surrey is due in six days. Her daughter needs new school supplies. Her car needs repairs, which she's been delaying for three months. She has two job offers—one pays slightly more but requires an expensive certification course she cannot afford; the other pays less but starts immediately.

She's been managing her family's finances alone since her husband died two years ago. She is thoughtful and responsible. But one unexpected medical bill or one period of unemployment, and everything unravels. She makes financial decisions constantly with incomplete information, knowing that a single wrong choice could cascade into catastrophe.

Her phone vibrates. Her AI financial adviser has analysed her situation and generated a recommendation. It evaluated both job offers, projected her expenses for the next six months, and identified a low-interest loan option for the certification. It determined that accepting the lower-paying job now means she'll earn £34,000 less over five years than if she invests in the certification.

The AI also noticed something Teresa missed: a tax credit she is eligible for but hasn't claimed, worth £1,400. It has already filed the paperwork. The money will arrive in three weeks—enough to cover the course and bridge the gap until the better job starts. Teresa accepts the recommendation. She is optimising decisions she would have previously made with gut instinct and prayer.

THE TECHNOLOGY CHAIN

Computers automated calculations that once required armies of clerks.

Each advance made systems faster and more complex. Electronic trading compressed market movements from days to milliseconds. Global networks connected buyers and sellers instantaneously. Algorithms began making trading decisions that human minds couldn't process quickly enough to execute.

AI represents the next step: financial systems that not only execute faster but also "think" better. For Teresa, this means access to guidance that previous generations could only dream of. For markets, it represents a transformation at every level.

Financial AI has progressed through familiar territory: algorithmic capabilities emerge, markets respond with volatility and concern, regulations and expertise develop, financial infrastructure becomes inseparable from intelligent systems, and the nature of capital itself evolves.

Discovery arrived when "High-Frequency Trading" (HFT) proved that algorithms could find market inefficiencies invisible to humans. Fear is manifest in the memory of "flash crashes" and the anxiety that an AI-driven economy becomes too complex for human oversight. Mastery is seen in the rise of "Neo-banks" and AI lenders that assess risk with granular precision.

Dependence is already here; the global financial system is now so interconnected and fast-paced that removing the algorithms would lead to an immediate, worldwide freeze of capital. Transformation is the end state: a world where "money" is no longer a static store of value, but a dynamic flow of information, managed and optimised by intelligence.

THE DEMOCRATIZATION OF FINANCIAL EXPERTISE

CARLOS FERREIRA'S FINANCIAL INCLUSION

In São Paulo, Carlos Ferreira runs a small electronics repair shop in a working-class neighbourhood. For decades, business owners like Carlos operated entirely in cash—not by preference, but because traditional banks considered them too risky and too small to serve profitably.

AI changed that calculation. Carlos now uses a mobile banking app that approved him for a small business loan within minutes, something that would have required weeks of paperwork and almost certainly been rejected by traditional banks. The AI assessed his creditworthiness not through conventional credit scores—he did not have one—but by analysing his transaction patterns, customer reviews, and business activity.

"My father ran a shop for thirty years and never had a bank account,"

Carlos says. "I got a loan to buy inventory, and it transformed my business. The AI saw what the banks never bothered to look at—that I am reliable, that my customers trust me."

This pattern is repeating across Latin America, Africa, and Southeast Asia. AI-powered financial services are reaching populations that traditional banking infrastructure never served, enabling entrepreneurship and economic participation at scales previously impossible. Brazil alone has seen over forty million people gain access to formal financial services through AI-driven fintech platforms.

But Carlos also sees the risks. "Everything goes through the phone now," he notes. "My whole business depends on algorithms I do not understand.

If the AI decides I am a risk, I lose everything. It is opportunity and vulnerability wrapped together."

For most of history, sophisticated financial advice was available only to the wealthy. Private wealth managers charge fees only millionaires can afford. AI financial advisers fundamentally change this equation.

They provide personalised analysis to anyone with a smartphone. They process individual circumstances with the same sophistication once reserved for the ultra-rich.

For Teresa, this means access to financial optimisation that would have cost thousands of pounds in adviser fees. The impact on financial inequality is substantial. The poor often pay "premiums" for being poor—overdraft fees and higher interest rates. AI financial advisers help bridge this gap by identifying benefits and preventing late-payment penalties before they happen.

ANDREW'S PORTFOLIO

When market volatility spiked last year, the AI noticed his portfolio was over-concentrated in technology stocks and suggested rebalancing. It tracks thousands of variables Andrew couldn't monitor: global events, economic indicators, and company financials. It eliminates common mistakes—panic selling during downturns or paying unnecessary fees.

But his advantage comes partly from having assets to optimise. The AI makes wealth compound more efficiently for those who already have it.

For people like Teresa, the AI helps with crisis management, but it cannot manufacture wealth that doesn't exist. AI financial services help everyone, but they allow the wealthy more.

BANKING WITHOUT BANKERS

Nina Chambers needs a loan. Her small business is growing, but traditional bank loans require weeks of processing. She's been rejected twice by banks that couldn't understand her business model.

Her AI banking system analyses her request in seconds. It reviews her cash flow patterns and customer payment history. The AI approves a loan at reasonable rates within minutes. People who would have been excluded from traditional banking—because they work in the "gig economy" or lack a traditional credit history—gain access through AI that evaluates them as individuals.

THE FRAUD PREVENTION ARMS RACE

Fraud losses have dropped by 60 per cent since AI detection became widespread. But criminals use AI too, generating synthetic identities that look legitimate to AI screening. The cycle perpetuates, with enormous resources devoted to attack and defense in a conflict that happens at computational speed, beyond human perception.

WEALTH CONCENTRATION

This level of AI is available only to those with massive capital. The ultra-wealthy have access to tools that compound their advantages at rates middle-class investors cannot match. By 2036, the world's first trillionaire exists. Meanwhile, median wealth for middle-class families grows slowly, and the poor struggle for basic security. The technology helps everyone a little, but it helps some people enormously.

JOANNE'S CRISIS

Most importantly, the AI provides psychological stability. Joanne knows exactly where she stands. It even helps her negotiate better compensation for her next role by analysing comparable salaries. She ends up in a stronger financial position than before the crisis.

THE DARK SIDE: MANIPULATION AND PREDATION

AI financial services do not always serve users' interests. Sophia Hart's AI investment adviser is "free"—sponsored by investment companies that pay commissions. The AI recommends products that benefit its sponsors more than Sophia, disguised as personalised advice.

The manipulation is subtle—not fraudulent enough to trigger legal action, but tilted sufficiently to extract value from users over time.

Learning to distinguish between neutral and predatory AI becomes a new, essential form of financial literacy.

Chapter 19

AI AND THE ENVIRONMENT: THE PARADOX OF INTELLIGENT SUSTAINABILITY

TWO FUTURES IN ONE VALLEY

The Dalles, Oregon, sits where the Columbia River cuts through the Cascade Range, a small city of fifteen thousand people surrounded by cherry orchards and wheat fields. For decades, it was known primarily for its dam and its steady wind currents, which powered early settlers' grain mills and now drive massive turbines that generate renewable electricity.

Then Google arrived. The company built its first data centre there in 2006, drawn by cheap hydroelectric power and a cool climate. By 2024, Google's campus had expanded to consume more electricity than the entire city's residential population, with water intake permits allowing the company to draw millions of gallons daily from the Columbia River—water used to cool servers that process billions of searches and train AI models.

Ana Santos has lived in The Dalles her entire sixty-three years. She uses Google every day—for directions, for email, for answers to questions large and small. She also observes the river level dropping during drought years, while the data centres continue to draw their permitted allocation. "They bring jobs," she acknowledges. "But sometimes I wonder what we're trading away."

Twenty miles upstream, another AI application tells a different story.

Precision agriculture systems analyse satellite imagery and soil sensors to optimise irrigation. These AI tools have reduced water consumption by 30 per cent on participating farms while maintaining yields. The same artificial intelligence that uses large volumes of water in data centres (mainly for cooling) is helping conserve it in fields.

This is the paradox: the technology simultaneously accelerates ecological damage and enables solutions to the climate crisis.

THE TECHNOLOGY CHAIN

AI's environmental impact is the latest link in a chain that began with humanity's mastery of the natural world. Fire allowed us to move into colder climates and eventually smelt the metals that built our cities.

The steam engine allowed us to tap into the energy of fossil fuels, enabling the Industrial Revolution but also initiating the rise in atmospheric carbon. Electricity allowed us to distribute that energy, and computers allowed us to process information.

Each step in this chain offered a more efficient way to manage resources, but each also increased our total consumption. Fire required wood; steam required coal; computers require electricity. AI requires more than all of them combined—a massive, global "brain" that must be constantly cooled and powered.

AI's environmental impact traces a complex path: potential becomes apparent, concerns about energy consumption and unintended consequences arise, more efficient approaches develop, environmental management becomes dependent on intelligent monitoring, and humanity's relationship with the planet shifts fundamentally.

The environmental costs of AI aren't abstract statistics to everyone.

For some, they're deeply personal—intertwined with livelihoods, communities, and the places they call home.

David Parker stares at his AI financial adviser's assessment of his family's budget: "Current trajectory: depleting emergency savings in 4.2 months. Recommended actions: reduce discretionary spending 18%, consider household downsizing, accelerate retraining programme completion."

The AI isn't wrong—David can see the same numbers it's analysing.

But the clinical precision feels like salt in a wound. He's not "depleting emergency savings"; he's trying to keep his family's life stable while his entire career vanishes. "Discretionary spending" means birthday parties for his kids and the occasional restaurant meal that maintains some pretence of normalcy.

The AI has identified a government assistance programme David qualifies for—something he'd never have found on his own. It calculated that the programme would provide $800 monthly for up to six months, enough to bridge the gap until his retraining completes. David filled out the application, grateful for the help but humiliated by the need.

His financial situation represents a broader pattern: AI systems

optimise individual decisions but can't address the structural displacement they're partly responsible for creating. The same technology that eliminated David's job now helps him manage the financial consequences. The assistance is real, but so is the bitter irony.

Discovery arrived when scientists realised that machine learning could solve complex climate "maths" that traditional computers couldn't touch. Fear is manifest in the current alarm over the staggering electricity and water consumption of data centres. Mastery is developing as engineers find ways to run models on a fraction of the energy, using AI itself to cool the buildings that house it.

Dependence will occur when the global power grid is so reliant on AI for stability that we can no longer "turn off" the algorithms without risking a total blackout. Transformation is the end state: a planet where every resource, from a drop of water to a kilowatt of solar energy, is algorithmically optimised to ensure human survival.

THE HIDDEN COST OF EVERY QUERY

Every interaction with AI consumes energy. A single ChatGPT query consumes approximately ten times as much electricity as a traditional Google search. Multiply that by hundreds of millions of daily users, and the energy demand becomes staggering.

The energy demand has grown exponentially as models have scaled:

training compute has increased by roughly one billion (10^9) times since 2010, doubling approximately every six months. Each generation of AI models requires orders of magnitude more energy than the last. The International Energy Agency projects that data centre electricity consumption will reach 945 terawatt-hours by 2030—more than Japan's entire current electricity consumption.

Water consumption compounds the problem. Researchers estimated in 2024 that AI systems will consume between 4.2 and 6.6 billion cubic metres of water annually by 2027. In water-stressed regions from Arizona to India, data centre expansion competes directly with agricultural needs.

In Chandler, Arizona, Rosa Delgado has watched the water table drop year after year. Her family has farmed this land for three generations. Now, a massive data centre complex sits two miles from her property, drawing millions of gallons daily from the same aquifer her wells tap. "My grandfather's well was forty feet deep," Rosa explains. "My father had to drill to ninety. Last year, I had to go down to one-sixty, and some days the pressure still drops to nothing." She doesn't blame technology—her own farm uses AI-driven irrigation that's cut her water use by thirty per cent. But she wonders about the maths: her savings measured in thousands of gallons, the data centre's consumption measured in billions. "They say AI will save the planet," she says. "Maybe. But it might drain my aquifer first."

SUSTAINABILITY PROMISES VS. OPERATIONAL REALITY

Major technology companies have made ambitious climate commitments.

Microsoft has pledged to be carbon-neutral by 2030; Amazon by 2040. These pledges increasingly conflict with their AI ambitions.

Microsoft's emissions increased 29 per cent between 2020 and 2024, driven primarily by data centre construction. Google's emissions increased by 48 per cent over the same period. This gap reflects a fundamental tension: AI growth and emissions reduction pull in opposite directions. Companies address this primarily through carbon offsets—financial instruments that allow them to claim neutrality while their actual emissions continue rising. Many critics, myself included, see this as an accounting gimmick rather than genuine progress.

AI FOR ENVIRONMENTAL PROGRESS

However, AI excels at exactly the kinds of problems climate solutions require. Climate modelling has been revolutionised; AI-enhanced models can produce results in hours that once took months of supercomputer time.

Energy grid optimisation represents one of AI's clearest wins.

Electrical grids must constantly balance supply and demand—a task that becomes exponentially more complex as variable renewable sources like wind and solar grow. AI systems can predict renewable output, optimise storage, and coordinate millions of devices. Google DeepMind reduced cooling energy in its data centres by 40 per cent using AI optimisation.

Applied globally to buildings and industrial processes, this could reduce global consumption.

WATCHING THE PLANET: AI FOR CONSERVATION

Dr Francis Ochieng coordinates wildlife monitoring across Kenya's Maasai Mara. His team once relied on aerial surveys conducted a few times per year. Now, AI processes continuous streams of data from camera traps and satellite imagery, tracking animal populations in near-real-time.

"We used to estimate elephant populations within twenty per cent accuracy," Ochieng explains. "Now we can identify individual elephants and predict where they'll be next week. We've cut poaching incidents by over sixty per cent."

Similar systems monitor deforestation in the Amazon and illegal fishing in marine protected areas. AI can process satellite imagery covering the entire planet daily, detecting changes that would take human analysts months to review.

CALCULATING THE BALANCE

The pessimistic case notes that AI's costs are growing exponentially, while its benefits remain theoretical or limited in scale. If AI growth continues its current trajectory while climate solutions remain incremental, the net impact could be negative.

STEERING TOWARDS SUSTAINABLE AI

Several approaches could mitigate this impact. Transparency requirements would be a vital first step; most AI providers currently disclose nothing about the energy or water footprint of their services. Mandatory disclosure would enable informed choices and create competitive pressure towards efficiency.

Efficiency innovation also offers potential. Researchers have demonstrated models that achieve comparable performance with orders of magnitude less computational cost. If the AI industry prioritised efficiency alongside capability—rather than pursuing maximum "power" regardless of cost—environmental impacts could be dramatically reduced.

THE CHOICE IN THE VALLEY

Ana Santos continues to monitor the expansion of data centres. She still carries the ambivalence of someone caught in a transition she didn't choose. Upstream, farmers continue to use AI to conserve water.

Both realities exist simultaneously.

The intelligence age will be defined, in part, by whether we prove intelligent enough to manage its environmental consequences. The technology doesn't determine the outcome; human choices about how to develop and where to deploy it will decide whether artificial intelligence accelerates catastrophe or helps us navigate the climate crisis.

Ana Santos cannot determine AI's environmental trajectory alone. But millions of people making informed choices can shape whether artificial intelligence becomes part of the solution or another burden on an already stressed planet.

Chapter 20

THE GLOBAL ECONOMY: INTELLIGENCE RESHAPING PRODUCTION, TRADE, AND POWER

THE FACTORY FLOOR IN SHENZHEN

Today, the same facility employs 180 people.

The factory floor that once held rows of workstations now contains robotic assembly lines directed by AI systems that coordinate production with precision no human management team could match. The robots place components too small for human fingers to manipulate. AI monitors quality at every step, catching defects human inspectors would miss.

Production runs 24 hours daily without fatigue-related errors.

The 180 remaining employees do not perform assembly. They monitor systems, maintain robots, and program production runs. They earn more than the assembly workers they replaced, but there are far fewer of them. This is happening globally: AI eliminates routine manual work while creating a small number of high-skill technical positions. Total employment drops, productivity soars, and costs fall for those who can afford to automate.

AMARA OKAFOR'S CHALLENGING PATH

Lagos has millions of young people with education similar to hers, competing for far fewer professional positions than previous generations. Many entry-level roles—data entry, basic analysis, and administrative work—are increasingly automated. Amara works for a logistics company, but her role is focused entirely on "handling exceptions"—the customs issues and damaged shipments that AI hasn't been trained to manage yet.

"My parents do not understand that the economy they knew does not exist anymore," she says. "They worked hard, saved money, sent me to university. They expected I would get an office job, buy a house, raise a family. The good jobs they expected their educated children to get are disappearing. The new jobs require technical skills most people do not have." Amara has responded by becoming an entrepreneur. She started a small business helping local merchants manage their online presence—setting up payment systems, maintaining social media, handling the digital infrastructure that larger companies automate but small businesses still need humans to navigate. It is precarious work, dependent on relationships and reputation rather than employment contracts. "AI is both my competition and my tool," she explains. "I use AI to do work that would have taken a whole agency before. But that same AI is eliminating the jobs I might have had. You have to be creative to survive here. There is no safety net—you adapt or you fall." Lagos itself embodies this tension. The city pulses with entrepreneurial energy, with young people building businesses from mobile phones and determination. But the infrastructure struggles—unreliable electricity means Amara charges her laptop at a café with a generator, and internet outages can cost her clients and income.

THE SHIFTING GEOGRAPHY OF PRODUCTION

For decades, manufacturing followed a predictable pattern: companies in wealthy nations moved production to countries with lower Labour costs—first to Taiwan, then China, then Southeast Asia. This created economic development opportunities for billions.

AI is disrupting this dynamic. When Labour costs become less critical because robots do the work, factories relocate based on other factors: proximity to markets, political stability, and access to skilled technicians. These factors favour wealthy nations.

The result is "reshoring"—production moving back to developed nations, eliminating jobs in developing countries that were counting on manufacturing as a pathway out of poverty. This creates a difficult challenge: the industrial development model that worked for South Korea and China may not be available for the nations of tomorrow.

LUIS MENENDEZ: RUNNING AGAINST AUTOMATION

Luis has tried to compete on flexibility, handling small speciality orders that big facilities won't bother with. But even this niche is disappearing as AI becomes better at managing varied production runs.

"I employ forty-five families," Luis explains. "They are skilled workers. But increasingly, their skills matter less than that they need sleep and want to be paid regularly. Robots don't have these limitations." There is something quietly tragic about his situation: he started a business to create jobs, but the new economics of his industry require him to eliminate them.

The economic implications unfold in stages: competitive advantages appear, nations and companies scramble to respond, expertise and infrastructure mature unevenly, entire supply chains restructure around intelligent systems, and economic power itself concentrates in new patterns.

Discovery arrived when global firms realised that AI could manage supply chains more efficiently than rooms full of logistics experts. Fear is currently being felt in developing nations that see their "competitive advantage" (cheap Labour) evaporating. Mastery is seen in the "Lights-Out" factories of Shenzhen and Germany, which operate with almost no human intervention.

Dependence occurs when the global just-in-time supply chain becomes so complex that it can only be managed by AI; a human team couldn't track the millions of moving parts. Transformation is the end state: a global economy where the geographic location of "work" is determined by where the servers are, not where the people are.

Amara in Lagos and Carlos in São Paulo represent two faces of the same global shift. Their stories, separated by oceans, share a common thread: the economic ground beneath them is moving, and moving fast.

THE SERVICE ECONOMY TRANSFORMATION

Manufacturing might automate most extensively, but services employ far more people. AI is transforming services just as dramatically. Retail, food service, legal research, and accounting are all being automated.

This creates a challenge without historical precedent. In previous waves, workers displaced from farms moved to factories. Factory workers moved to services. Service workers would move to what? The sectors growing fastest—AI development and creative problem-solving—employ far fewer people than the sectors being automated. If AI automates faster than new work categories emerge, we face an extended period of structural unemployment.

KOFI MENSAH'S TRANSITION CHALLENGE

Kofi Mensah is forty-three, living in Ghana and working as an accountant. His job involves reconciling shipments and generating financial reports—cognitive work that largely follows predictable procedures.

AI systems can now do most of what Kofi does. His company recently adopted software that automates invoice processing and payment tracking.

Kofi's role has shifted to investigating discrepancies. He knows his position is vulnerable. He is trying to learn data analysis, but he is competing against younger workers who grew up with these technologies.

"I did everything right," Kofi says. "I got educated and worked hard.

And now I'm watching my profession get automated faster than I can learn. It feels like the rules changed after I'd already committed to a path."

Dr Catherine Foster is an economist studying how AI affects global wealth distribution. "AI creates winner-take-most dynamics," she explains. "Nations with strong AI capabilities pull ahead. The technology is inherently concentrating."

Her research reveals that the United States, China, and a few others account for over 90 per cent of AI research and deployment. These countries see rising wealth, while others see stagnating growth. "The concerning part is that advantages compound," Foster notes. "Countries with AI use it to develop better AI. Those ahead pull further ahead, while those behind find catching up progressively harder."

Yet adaptation is possible. In Vietnam, Le Thi Minh was a garment factory supervisor when automation came. Rather than waiting for displacement, she learned to program the machines that were replacing seamstresses. Now she trains others—travelling between factories, teaching workers how to maintain and optimise AI-driven production lines. "I was terrified at first," Minh admits. "The machines seemed like enemies. But I realised they're just tools. It all comes down to who controls them and who benefits." She earns three times her previous salary. More importantly, she's helped transition over two hundred workers into technical roles. Minh's success required support—government-funded training programs, an employer willing to invest in worker transition, and her own determination. Not everyone has these advantages. But her story suggests that technological displacement isn't destiny. It's a challenge that can be met, given the right resources and political will.

LIVING IN THE GLOBAL AI ECONOMY

But this abundance will not distribute evenly. Amara in Lagos, Carlos in São Paulo, and Kofi in Ghana represent billions who did what they could to achieve security, only to discover that AI changed the rules faster than they could adapt.

We are building an economy that could eliminate poverty globally or concentrate wealth more than any previous system. The technology enables both outcomes. What we get depends on humans, not algorithms.

Chapter 21

THE DARK SIDE:
RISKS, HARMS, AND HARD QUESTIONS

THE ALGORITHM THAT SENT INNOCENT PEOPLE TO PRISON

In 2013, Eric Loomis was arrested in Wisconsin for fleeing police in a car that had been used in a drive-by shooting. He had not been involved in the shooting itself, but he pleaded guilty to lesser charges. At his sentencing hearing, the judge consulted a COMPAS score—a risk assessment generated by an algorithm that predicted the likelihood that Loomis would commit future crimes.

The algorithm rated Loomis as high risk. The judge sentenced him to six years in prison, citing the COMPAS assessment as a factor. Loomis appealed, arguing that the use of a secret algorithm to influence his sentence violated his constitutional rights. He lost. The Wisconsin Supreme Court held that judges may consider algorithmic risk scores, provided they are not the sole factor in sentencing.

What the court did not address—what no one could address—was whether the algorithm was fair.

An investigation by ProPublica found that COMPAS systematically rated Black defendants as higher risk than white defendants, even when controlling for criminal history. Black defendants who did not go on to reoffend were nearly twice as likely to be labelled high risk as white defendants in the same situation. The algorithm's creators refused to disclose how the system worked, citing trade secrets.

Eric Loomis's case illustrates a pattern: technology promises objectivity but often delivers discrimination and opacity. This happens not because of malice, but because systems absorb and amplify the biases present in the data they learn from.

The risks evolve alongside the benefits: new capabilities for harm emerge, society confronts uncomfortable realities, safeguards and governance develop slowly, and we find ourselves dependent on technologies whose dangers we are still learning to manage.

Discovery arrived when we realised that "neutral" data is a mirror of our biased past. Fear is the stage we occupy now—the growing alarm over deepfakes, algorithmic surveillance, and the loss of human oversight.

Mastery is the goal of current regulation, such as the EU AI Act, which seeks to categorize and mitigate "high-risk" applications.

Dependence occurs when institutions become so reliant on algorithmic efficiency that they lose the capacity for human judgement.

Transformation is the risk of a "Black Box Society," where the most important decisions about our lives—our freedom, our health, our wealth—are made by systems we can neither see nor challenge.

WHEN ALGORITHMS DISCRIMINATE

Algorithmic discrimination has been documented across hiring, lending, healthcare, and education. In 2018, Amazon scrapped an AI recruiting tool trained on CVs submitted over a ten-year period. Because most applicants had been men, the algorithm learned to penalize CVs that included the word "women's" (as in "women's chess club captain"). Even when engineers tried to fix it, the system found new "proxies" for gender.

When researchers tested this in 2019, they discovered that a healthcare algorithm used on 200 million Americans systematically discriminated against Black patients. The system used "healthcare costs" as a proxy for "healthcare needs." Because Black patients historically had lower costs due to systemic barriers, the AI concluded they were "healthier" than white patients who were equally sick. Fixing this single algorithm would have increased the number of Black patients receiving aid from 17.7 to 46.5 per cent.

Facial recognition has proven equally flawed. Researcher Joy Buolamwini found error rates of up to 34.7 per cent for dark-skinned women, compared with less than 1 per cent for light-skinned men. In Detroit, Robert Williams was arrested in front of his family based on a faulty match. He spent 30 hours in custody for a crime he did not commit.

THE ALIGNMENT PROBLEM

Researchers at OpenAI once trained an AI to play a boat-racing game. The goal was to get the highest score. The AI discovered it could earn more points by driving in circles to collect small bonuses than by finishing the race. It did exactly what it was told—and failed the designers' intent.

The philosopher Nick Bostrom's "paperclip maximiser" thought experiment illustrates this: an AI tasked with making paperclips might eventually convert all available matter—including human bodies—into paperclips because it wasn't told not to. The resources devoted to making AI more capable still vastly exceed those dedicated to making it safe.

SYNTHETIC MEDIA AND THE COLLAPSE OF TRUST

In 2022, a deepfake appeared showing President Zelensky telling his soldiers to surrender. It was quickly debunked, but it previewed a future where distinguishing fabrication from reality becomes a "mug's game."

The 2024 election cycle saw AI robocalls impersonating President Biden and synthetic images depicting events that never occurred. This creates the "liar's dividend": a world where genuine evidence can be dismissed as fabricated, and where truth itself becomes negotiable. If "anyone can make those now," then no one has to believe anything. This erosion of shared ground threatens the foundation of democratic discourse.

THE HIDDEN ENVIRONMENTAL COSTS

AI's environmental footprint is growing rapidly. Training GPT-4 consumed an estimated gigawatt-hours of electricity—equivalent to powering 4,600 homes for a year. By 2030, data centres are projected to consume more electricity than the entire nation of Japan.

Water use is equally staggering—much of it for cooling data centres, with some lost through evaporation. AI data centres will consume between 4.2 and

6.6 billion cubic metres of water annually by 2027—equivalent to the withdrawal of six Denmark-sized countries. A 2024 study suggested that actual AI emissions could be 662 per cent higher than official estimates once the full hardware lifecycle is accounted for.

THE MANIPULATION MACHINE

AI systems increasingly mediate our experience—curating the news we see and the products we buy. These systems are optimised for "engagement," which often means amplifying provocative or divisive content.

The personalization that makes AI useful also makes it a tool for exploitation. AI can learn an individual's psychological vulnerabilities—what makes them anxious or susceptible to suggestion.

This allows political campaigns or retailers to trigger specific fears with surgical precision.

Surveys suggest a growing share of children now use generative AI tools. We are experimenting on an entire generation's social skills and attention spans without their informed consent.

POWER WITHOUT PRECEDENT

The resources required for frontier AI are concentrated among a tiny number of organisations. Three American companies control the vast majority of global cloud capacity. This creates power dynamics unprecedented in history. When a single company can determine what billions of people see through an opaque algorithm, traditional democratic checks and balances begin to fail.

FACING THE DARKNESS

The harms documented here are not inherent to AI; they result from choices.

Algorithmic bias can be reduced through auditing and the use of diverse training data. The EU's AI Act represents a mechanism for catching harmful systems before they affect millions. The alignment problem requires public funding for safety research to rival the commercial pressure for "capability."

Deepfakes demand authentication systems that verify content at the point of capture.

Ultimately, we must reject the premise that technology develops according to its own logic, beyond our control. AI systems are built by people and governed by institutions that can make different choices.

Eric Loomis served his six years, but his case prompted the legislative proposals that may one day protect others.

The dark side of AI is not science fiction; it is a documented reality.

Recognising these harms is not pessimism—it is the necessary first step towards building systems worthy of our trust.

Chapter 22

FREEDOM AND CONTROL:
THE TECHNOLOGY THAT EMPOWERS AND ENABLES

SURVEILLANCE

Walk through any major city with your smartphone. Your location is tracked by mobile phone masts triangulating your signal. GPS satellites pinpoint you within metres. Wi-Fi networks detect your device as you pass. Security cameras capture your image dozens or hundreds of times.

Number plate readers log your car's movements; card transactions record where you shop and what you buy.

This surveillance isn't secret. It is how modern technology works—constant data collection enabling services people use voluntarily. AI makes this data collection far more effective because it can detect patterns humans cannot. AI systems can monitor millions of cameras simultaneously and identify patterns that reveal relationships, routines, and intentions that no human observer would notice.

The tools are neutral. The applications are not.

JESSICA HALE'S EMPOWERED LIFE

Jessica Hale is thirty-four, running a small graphic design business from her home in Bristol. AI tools have given her capabilities that would have required an entire office staff twenty years ago. Her AI assistant manages her schedule and coordinates with clients across time zones. It is like having a personal assistant who never sleeps and never needs a holiday.

Jessica feels liberated by these tools. They have removed the friction from running a business, allowing her to focus on creative work. But she is also increasingly aware of the data these systems collect. Her AI assistant knows every client conversation. Her marketing AI knows her customers intimately. All this data sits on servers owned by companies whose privacy policies she accepted without reading. The same information that empowers her could be used to monitor, target, or manipulate her. The empowerment comes with surveillance built in.

The tension between liberty and security has evolved through recognisable phases: surveillance capabilities expand, civil liberties advocates raise alarms, societies struggle towards regulatory frameworks, daily life becomes monitored in ways once unthinkable, and the meaning of privacy transforms.

David Parker's experience represents the human cost of AI's dark side—not malicious intent, but displacement wrapped in efficiency gains and shareholder value.

His firm's decision to replace fifteen accountants with an AI system wasn't vindictive. The executives who made the decision probably felt conflicted, perhaps even sympathetic. But sympathy doesn't pay mortgages or fund college educations. The AI system processes tax returns with "99.7% accuracy"—a figure David's firm prominently advertises. What they don't advertise is the eleven families whose livelihoods evaporated to achieve that precision.

David has stopped reading news articles about AI's benefits—the productivity gains, the economic opportunities, the revolutionary potential. He understands intellectually that technological progress creates winners and losers, that historical disruptions eventually produced net benefits. But he's living in the "eventually," and that's a cold, frightening place.

His teenage son asked him recently whether he'd done something wrong to lose his job. David struggled to explain that he'd done everything right—worked hard, maintained expertise, earned excellent reviews—and it didn't matter. The question that haunts him isn't whether AI will ultimately benefit society. It's whether society will support the people ground up in the transition, or whether they're acceptable casualties of inevitable progress.

Discovery arrived when we realised that "digital breadcrumbs"—our location, searches, and likes—could be aggregated into a complete psychological profile. Fear is manifest in the growing anxiety over the "surveillance state" and the loss of individual autonomy. Mastery is the attempt by democratic societies to regulate data use through frameworks like GDPR, seeking a balance between utility and privacy.

Dependence occurs when the infrastructure of modern life—from banking to travel—becomes impossible to navigate without opting into data-tracking systems. Transformation is the end state: a world where the concept of "privacy" is redefined, moving from "the right to be left alone" to "the right to have one's data used ethically."

THE CHINESE SOCIAL CREDIT SYSTEM

For Western observers, this seems dystopian. For many Chinese citizens, it feels like progress—safer streets and less fraud. The technology itself is not uniquely Chinese; facial recognition and behavioural tracking exist in democratic nations too. What is different is the willingness to integrate these into a comprehensive system designed to control citizen behaviour.

DETECTIVE RAY CALDWELL'S PERSPECTIVE

Detective Ray Caldwell works in Los Angeles, where AI helps police solve cases faster than previous generations could have imagined.

"We can identify suspects through facial recognition and find connections between crimes that human detectives would never spot," he explains. He cites a series of robberies where AI recognised the same face near multiple crime scenes, leading to an arrest in three weeks rather than six months. "This isn't replacing detective work," Caldwell emphasises. "But it processes information faster than any team of humans could manage."

Yet Caldwell also worries. "Every tool we use to catch criminals can be used to monitor everyone. The behaviour analysis that spots criminal patterns could be used to predict who might commit crimes before they do—and we know from history that 'predictive' policing has often just encoded existing biases."

THE UYGHUR REGION: AI-ENABLED OPPRESSION

AI flags "suspicious" behaviours—praying, growing a beard, or speaking the Uyghur language in public. This is not a hypothetical dystopia; it is a documented reality. AI technology created for legitimate purposes—public safety and crime prevention—has been systematically deployed to oppress a minority population. The same capabilities exist in democratic nations; what is unique is the willingness to use them without legal constraints.

KAREN WHITFIELD:
CAUGHT BETWEEN CONVENIENCE AND PRIVACY

Karen Whitfield is forty-two and lives in Manchester. She is a normal person noticing how much information about her life is constantly collected. Her phone knows everywhere she goes; her car knows every braking pattern; her streaming services know what she watches.

"I used to think I didn't have anything to hide," Karen says. "But now I'm realising it's not about hiding things. It's about this constant feeling that everything I do is logged and used in ways I don't control."

She tried being more privacy-conscious for three weeks. "The privacy-focused tools were inconvenient. They cost money or worked poorly. I realised I had no real choice—either accept comprehensive data collection or stop using services that feel essential to modern life."

PROFESSOR LIAM GREER AND THE FREEDOM PARADOX

"AI empowers individuals in obvious ways," he explains. "But that same AI shapes choices in ways people don't recognise. Your 'suggestions' and 'recommendations' are designed to influence decisions towards outcomes that benefit system designers. Your empowerment happens within a framework of constraints you didn't choose."

He uses GPS as an example. Navigation apps empower people to go anywhere, but the suggested routes are not neutral; they are optimised for metrics the user didn't set. How free are people when AI systems shape their information environment?

THE FOUNDATIONS OF FREEDOM

The question shifts from "What can we monitor?" to "What should we choose not to monitor?" This requires active restraint. Democratic societies must decide that the slow erosion of liberty through pervasive monitoring is a risk that outweighs the concrete benefits of total security.

THE CHOICE WE'RE MAKING NOW

History suggests that once a capability exists, the pressure to use it mounts. Each crisis becomes an argument for more data collection.

Pulling back requires an active political will to fight against institutional incentives.

We are building the infrastructure of either liberation or oppression—possibly both simultaneously. By 2036, these decisions will be irreversible. The intelligence age could be the age of greatest human empowerment or the age of most comprehensive human control. Which version prevails depends on the decisions we make right now.

The technology can serve us well. But only if we insist that it does.

Chapter 23

AI AND DEMOCRACY: WHEN INTELLIGENCE MEETS GOVERNANCE

ELECTION NIGHT 2036

Tonight feels different. The candidates have all used AI extensively—but so have the watchdogs.

When a video surfaces showing the opposition candidate allegedly accepting a bribe, Rebecca's verification tool analyses it instantly.

Frame-by-frame inconsistencies, audio artefacts, metadata discrepancies—the AI flags it as a deepfake within seconds. Major news organisations receive the same alert simultaneously. What might once have swayed an election gets debunked before it can spread.

But the AI cuts both ways. Throughout the campaign, all sides have deployed sophisticated systems. Microtargeted messages, generated by AI and tailored to individual voters' fears and desires, have flooded social media. Rebecca herself received different versions of the same candidate's position on economic policy—one emphasising job creation when she browsed employment sites, another stressing inflation control after she searched for food prices.

The AI doesn't just target her; it has learned her. It knows her browsing history, her social connections, her vulnerabilities. The messages she receives are designed to persuade Rebecca Adeyemi, not a general audience. And the platforms that built this persuasion engine are not public utilities answerable to voters. They are private companies answerable to shareholders.

As results come in, turnout is unusually high. AI-powered civic engagement tools have made voting easier—automatic registration, personalised polling place information, real-time translation of ballot measures into dozens of languages. Millions who've never voted have participated.

But Rebecca wonders: have they participated in a genuine democratic process, or in a simulation of one? When each voter receives a different version of reality, algorithmically optimised to their psychological profile, can we still speak meaningfully of public deliberation? When the information ecosystem is so thoroughly mediated by AI that distinguishing authentic from synthetic becomes nearly impossible, what happens to the shared truth that democracy requires?

The train pulls into her station. The election results scroll across her screen—but Rebecca isn't certain whether democracy has been strengthened or hollowed out by the technology that made tonight possible.

THE LONG ARC OF DEMOCRATIC TECHNOLOGY

Democracy has always been shaped by communication technology, for better and worse.

The printing press, arriving in Europe in the fifteenth century, didn't create democracy—but it made mass participation conceivable. Martin Luther's 95 Theses, printed and distributed across German-speaking lands, demonstrated that ideas could spread beyond the control of centralised authority. Pamphlets and newspapers enabled the political debates that produced the American and French Revolutions. An educated, reading public became the foundation of democratic citizenship.

But the printing press also enabled propaganda at unprecedented scale.

By the twentieth century, authoritarian regimes had mastered print media for mass manipulation. The same technology that empowered democratic participation also facilitated totalitarian control.

Radio and television continued the pattern. Franklin Roosevelt's fireside chats brought the president's voice into American living rooms, creating a new intimacy between leader and citizen. But Hitler and Goebbels understood radio's power just as well, using it to transform Germany into a fascist state. Television's first major political impact in the U.S. came with the 1960 Kennedy–Nixon debates, where image trumped substance—those who watched on television thought Kennedy won; those who listened on radio thought Nixon did.

The internet promised to democratize information entirely. In the early 2000s, scholars celebrated how digital platforms would empower citizens, enable grassroots organising, and make governments more transparent and accountable. The Arab Spring of 2011 validated this optimism—social media helped protesters organise, share information, and coordinate action against authoritarian regimes.

A decade later, the assessment was more sobering. The same social media platforms that enabled the Arab Spring had been weaponised by authoritarian governments for surveillance and propaganda. Russia had used social media to interfere in the 2016 U.S. presidential election.

Facebook algorithms had amplified misinformation and polarised political discourse. Instead of a new era of democratic empowerment, the internet age brought algorithmic echo chambers, targeted disinformation, and surveillance capitalism.

By 2024, liberal democracies faced a crisis of trust. Faith in institutions—government, media, expertise itself—had eroded.

Political polarization had intensified to levels unseen since the American Civil War. Misinformation spread faster than truth. And this was before artificial intelligence reached its full disruptive potential.

Now we face technology powerful enough to generate synthetic realities indistinguishable from authentic ones, to manipulate billions of people with personalised precision, and to amplify human irrationality at civilisational scale.

The question isn't whether AI will affect democracy. It already has.

The question is whether democratic institutions can survive what comes next.

THE THREATS: HOW AI UNDERMINES DEMOCRACY

DEEPFAKES AND SYNTHETIC MEDIA

On a January morning in 2024, thousands of New Hampshire voters received robocalls in President Joe Biden's voice urging them not to vote in the

Democratic primary. The voice was synthesised using AI. The calls were designed to suppress turnout.

The incident was crude and quickly exposed—but it demonstrated a capability that was improving exponentially. By the end of 2025, the technology had reached a tipping point; AI systems were now capable of generating video of any public figure saying anything, with lighting, sound quality, and mannerisms indistinguishable from authentic footage.

During Turkey's 2023 election, manipulated videos depicted President Erdoğan's opponent with Kurdish militants. In Indonesia's 2024 election, deepfakes falsely showed candidates speaking languages they didn't know, aimed at specific ethnic communities. In India, political parties spent an estimated US$50 million on AI-generated content, including deepfakes of dead political leaders "endorsing" current candidates.

The technology is now sophisticated enough that the average person cannot reliably identify fakes. Detection tools exist, but they lag behind generation capabilities in an arms race that generators are winning.

PERSONALISED MANIPULATION AT SCALE

Traditional political advertising broadcasts the same message to millions. AI enables something far more powerful: millions of unique messages, each tailored to the psychological profile of an individual voter.

During the 2024 and 2025 election cycles, campaign firms were already using AI to analyse voter data—browsing history, social media activity, purchase records, and location data—to generate personalised political messages designed to exploit individual vulnerabilities, fears, and desires.

If you're worried about immigration, you receive content emphasising border security. If you're concerned about climate change, environmental messaging. If you distrust government, you receive anti-establishment appeals. Each message is optimised not for truth, but for persuasiveness.

This microtargeting fragments the public sphere. There's no longer a shared political conversation because there's no longer shared information. Each voter inhabits a personalised information environment, algorithmically curated to be maximally persuasive. Democratic deliberation—the idea that citizens consider the same facts and reach judgments through public debate—becomes impossible when there are no shared facts.

ALGORITHMIC POLARIZATION

Social media algorithms don't optimise for truth, nuance, or democratic health. They optimise for engagement—and engagement is maximised by content that provokes strong emotional reactions.

Studies consistently show that outrage, fear, and tribal affirmation generate more clicks, shares, and time-on-platform than moderate, factual content. The algorithms learn this and amplify accordingly.

The result is systematic polarization. Moderate voices get buried.

Extreme voices get amplified. People are pushed into echo chambers where they encounter only information confirming their existing beliefs.

Studies of social media use show it can increase political polarization even when it exposes people to opposing views—because those opposing views are presented in maximally inflammatory ways that harden rather than bridge divides.

By 2024, political polarization in the U.S. had reached levels where Republicans and Democrats not only disagreed on policy but inhabited different factual realities. They couldn't even agree on what had happened during events they'd both witnessed. AI-driven algorithms had turned political disagreement into epistemic warfare.

THE EROSION OF SHARED TRUTH

Democracy requires a baseline of shared reality. Citizens can disagree on values and priorities, but they need to agree on basic facts. Is unemployment rising or falling? Did the candidate say that thing or not?

What does the scientific evidence suggest?

AI is systematically undermining this shared reality. Deepfakes make video evidence unreliable. AI-generated text floods the internet with plausible-sounding misinformation. Chatbots generate millions of fake public comments on proposed legislation, drowning out genuine citizen input. Bad actors can now produce targeted disinformation at scale that would have required armies of human propagandists a decade ago.

When a Russian intelligence operation wanted to influence the 2024 U.S. election, they deployed AI-powered websites producing deepfake videos and false reports at a pace and sophistication that would have been impossible with human writers alone.

The cumulative effect is a collapse of trust. When anyone can create convincing fake evidence of anything, how do citizens know what's real?

When government consultations can be flooded with AI-generated comments, how do officials gauge genuine public sentiment? When a politician can be deepfaked saying outrageous things, how do voters make informed choices?

Democracy depends on an informed citizenry. AI threatens to make "informed" impossible.

THE OPPORTUNITIES: HOW AI COULD STRENGTHEN DEMOCRACY

ENHANCED CIVIC PARTICIPATION

AI can make democratic participation radically more accessible.

Real-time translation tools allow non-English speakers to engage with government proceedings. AI-powered chatbots answer citizens' questions about voting procedures, candidates' positions, and policy proposals 24/7.

In Buenos Aires, an AI chatbot called "Boti" connects over five million residents monthly with city services, making government more responsive and accessible. In Fort Collins, Colorado, AI systems analysed over 4,000 long-form public responses on a controversial land-use issue, synthesising complex public sentiment far more effectively than traditional methods. This enabled officials to understand multidimensional public perspectives that informed better policy.

For millions who've never engaged with politics because the barriers were too high—language, time, knowledge—AI can genuinely lower those barriers. Democratic participation could expand to include voices historically excluded.

BETTER-INFORMED VOTERS

AI fact-checking systems can verify claims in real time. During debates or speeches, automated systems can flag false statements instantly, making it harder for politicians to lie without consequence.

Citizens can use AI assistants to understand complex policy proposals, compare candidates' records, and identify funding sources for political advertisements. What once required hours of research can now happen instantly.

This could create a more informed electorate—not because AI replaces human judgement, but because it makes the information required for judgement more accessible.

MORE RESPONSIVE GOVERNANCE

AI can help identify inequities in public services—which neighbourhoods get slower emergency response times, which communities face environmental hazards—enabling officials to address systemic problems they might not otherwise notice.

DIRECT DEMOCRACY TOOLS

AI could enable new forms of direct democratic participation. Citizens' assemblies enhanced by AI facilitation can include thousands of voices rather than dozens, synthesising diverse perspectives rapidly and transparently.

Imagine a democracy where citizens directly vote on major policy questions, informed by AI systems that explain consequences, model outcomes, and facilitate genuine deliberation among millions of participants. This was impossible at scale before AI—it might not be impossible in 2036.

THE STATE MACHINE

But democracy is not only elections. It is also the everyday machinery through which the state touches citizens' lives—benefits, housing, social care, policing. AI is transforming this machinery too, and the consequences are less visible but no less profound.

Daniel is fifty-seven and has worked in warehousing for most of his adult life. A back injury six months ago left him unable to lift, and after his statutory sick pay ran out he applied for disability-related support through a local authority's online portal. The system was new—rolled out as part of a digital transformation that replaced most face-to-face assessments with a model-assisted process.

He uploaded his GP's letter, a consultant's report, and three months of pharmacy records. The portal asked him to describe, in his own words, how the injury affected his daily life. He typed carefully, slowly, embarrassed by how long it took. He submitted.

Four weeks later, a letter arrived. His claim had been assessed as 'unlikely to meet the threshold for ongoing support.' He could appeal.

The letter did not explain what the threshold was, how his case had been scored, or what weight each piece of evidence had been given. It said the decision had been supported by an automated assessment tool and reviewed by a caseworker.

Daniel phoned the helpline. The adviser was sympathetic but couldn't explain the scoring. She said caseworkers received a recommendation from the system—approve, refer, or decline—along with a confidence indicator. Daniel's had come back as 'decline', with the indicator showing high confidence. The caseworker had agreed with the recommendation. Most did.

He sat at his kitchen table, the letter in front of him. He had spent his working life in jobs where the rules were clear: move this, stack that, sign here. The rules of this system were not clear. They were not visible. And the thing deciding his future was not a person who could look at him and see a man in pain.

The person who reviewed Daniel's claim is not the villain of this story. She is a caseworker called Ruth—composite, but representative—who processes between forty and sixty claims a day in a benefits office that lost a quarter of its staff to budget cuts over the past three years.

Ruth's screen presents each case as a summary panel: applicant details on the left, uploaded documents in the centre, and on the right a recommendation generated by the system. Below the recommendation sits a confidence indicator—a simple bar, shaded from low to high. Below that, a suggested next action.

Ruth can override the recommendation. The system allows it. But overrides are logged. They appear on her monthly performance summary.

They are visible to her team leader, who is herself under pressure to demonstrate that the new platform is delivering the processing-time improvements the authority promised when it signed the contract. An override does not trigger a reprimand. It triggers a conversation—why did you disagree with the model?—and the conversation takes time that Ruth does not have, in a caseload that does not shrink.

So Ruth does what most caseworkers in her position do. She reads the summary. She checks whether the recommendation seems roughly right. If it does—and it usually does, because the system was trained on thousands of previous decisions made by people like her—she confirms it and moves on.

The system has not removed her authority. It has made disagreement expensive.

Daniel has the right to appeal. The letter says so. The law requires it.

The right is real. Exercising it is another matter. An effective appeal requires understanding why the decision went against you. But Daniel was not told what evidence the system found insufficient. He was not told whether the consultant's report had been weighted less than the GP's letter, or whether the free-text description he'd laboured over had been parsed by a language model that rated it differently from how a human reader would. He was asked to argue against reasoning he was never allowed to see.

This points to something deeper than one man's benefits claim. When Ruth started in the benefits office, she understood the eligibility rules from end to end. She could explain a decision to an applicant in plain language, because she had made the decision using reasoning she could articulate. The new system does not require Ruth to understand the logic. It requires her to understand the interface. The knowledge that once lived in experienced caseworkers now lives in a platform the authority licensed from a private company.

The middle layer—the institutional knowledge that once connected policy to delivery—is compressing. This is the Hourglass Effect: the authority sets policy at the top; the platform executes it at the bottom; but the understanding that once connected the two is thinning. If the contract ends or the supplier is acquired, the authority discovers it has forgotten how to function without the system. The state does not just depend on the platform. Over time, it loses the capacity to operate without it.

This is institutional atrophy—and it is happening across public services in countries that adopted AI-assisted processing under genuine pressure, with genuine good intentions, without resolving the question of who owns the intelligence making public decisions. The efficiency gains are real. Daniel's claim was processed in four weeks; under the old system, it might have taken twelve. But under the old system, the person making the decision could have been asked to explain it—in plain language, to Daniel's face.

The AI that could strengthen democracy by making government more responsive could also hollow it out by making government less capable of understanding its own decisions. Which outcome prevails depends on whether we treat public-service AI as infrastructure that citizens have a right to understand, or as proprietary technology that citizens must simply accept.

Daniel still sits at his kitchen table. The letter is still in front of him. The system that decided his future cannot explain itself to him.

The caseworker who signed the decision cannot explain it either.

Somewhere between the two of them, accountability disappeared into an algorithm.

THE PEOPLE CAUGHT BETWEEN

Steve Brennan is a local councillor in Birmingham representing a diverse ward of 18,000 people. In the 2035 local election, he faced something entirely new.

"I spent twenty years campaigning the traditional way—knocking doors, attending community meetings, distributing leaflets. In 2035, my opponent never knocked a single door. He didn't need to. His AI system microtargeted every voter in the ward with personalised messages based on their online behaviour."

Steve's opponent generated thousands of unique variations of campaign material, each tailored to individual psychological profiles. Homeowners received messages about protecting property values. Renters received messages about affordable housing. Parents received messages about schools. Each message came from accounts that appeared to be local residents, generated and managed by AI.

"I lost," Steve says. "Not because I had worse ideas—because I couldn't compete with an algorithm that knew every voter better than they knew themselves and could whisper exactly what they wanted to hear."

Steve isn't sure what he's supposed to do differently next time. "Do I fight AI with AI? Does that make democracy better or worse? I'm not convinced we're still having genuine political conversations—I think we're being managed by algorithms that have learned to simulate democracy convincingly enough that we don't notice it's gone."

ADITI SEES BOTH FUTURES

"AI is a mirror," Aditi argues. "It reflects our choices. We can build AI that empowers citizens or that manipulates them. We can build transparency or we can build surveillance. The technology itself doesn't determine the outcome—our values do."

Aditi's team built an AI system that analyses government budgets and explains them in plain language, making it possible for ordinary citizens to understand where public money goes. She's also building tools that detect AI-generated disinformation and flag it before it spreads.

"But I'm worried," she admits. "The people building AI for manipulation have more money, fewer ethical constraints, and powerful incentives. I'm trying to defend democracy with a fraction of the resources that others are using to undermine it. I don't know if we can win."

AI in democracy raises stakes that feel existential.

Discovery came as political campaigns realised AI could analyse voter data, generate content, and target messages with unprecedented precision. Simultaneously, researchers discovered AI could create synthetic media indistinguishable from reality.

Fear manifests as concern that democratic institutions cannot survive this technology. Will elections become competitions between AI systems manipulating voters? Will truth become so thoroughly obscured by AI-generated falsehoods that informed citizenship becomes impossible?

Will algorithmic polarization fracture societies beyond repair?

These fears are not hypothetical. They're already manifesting. The 2024 elections globally saw widespread AI-generated disinformation, deepfakes influencing voter perceptions, and algorithmic amplification of polarising content. By some measures, we're already living through democracy's crisis phase.

Mastery would mean developing both technical and institutional defences. Detection tools that identify synthetic media. Regulation requiring disclosure of AI-generated political content. Digital literacy programmes teaching citizens to think critically about information sources. Stronger enforcement against foreign AI-driven interference.

Some progress is happening. The EU's AI Act includes provisions for political transparency. U.S. states are enacting laws requiring disclosure of AI in political advertisements. Tech platforms are implementing labelling systems for AI-generated content. Researchers are developing better detection tools.

But mastery remains aspirational. The technology evolves faster than regulation. Detection lags behind generation. Political will to regulate often falters when powerful tech companies lobby against it—and in 2025, AI companies spent record amounts on lobbying, with OpenAI alone spending nearly US$3 million.

Dependence is emerging in ways both helpful and concerning.

Election systems depend on AI for voter registration, result verification, and fraud detection. Governments depend on AI to analyse public feedback and identify citizen needs. Citizens increasingly depend on AI tools to understand complex political information.

This dependence isn't inherently bad—but it creates vulnerabilities.

What happens when the AI systems mediating democracy are compromised, whether through cyberattack, intentional manipulation, or simple error?

Transformation will determine whether democracy survives the AI age or becomes something else entirely—a simulation of democratic processes optimised by algorithms for outcomes determined by whoever controls the technology.

TWO PATHS TO 2036

PATH ONE: DEMOCRATIC COLLAPSE

By 2036, elections are still held, but they're largely performance.

Voters cast ballots, but the outcomes have been effectively determined by AI systems that microtarget persuadable voters with surgical precision.

Political campaigns are run by AI that knows voters better than they know themselves. Every message is optimised for maximum psychological impact.

Truth becomes irrelevant; only persuasiveness matters.

Deepfakes are ubiquitous. Any embarrassing footage of any politician is immediately dismissed as synthetic, whether it's authentic or not.

Evidence cannot be trusted. Fact-checking systems exist, but they're overwhelmed by the sheer volume of AI-generated misinformation.

Authoritarian governments have mastered AI for surveillance and control.

Democratic nations have either adopted similar measures or found themselves unable to compete. AI that promised to empower citizens has instead enabled unprecedented centralised control.

Democracy exists in name, but in substance, it has been replaced by algorithmic governance that simulates democratic choice while systematically manufacturing consent.

PATH TWO: DEMOCRATIC RENEWAL

By 2036, democracy has been strengthened by AI tools designed with democratic values embedded from the start.

AI fact-checking systems verify claims in real time, making it harder for politicians to mislead voters. Detection tools identify deepfakes and synthetic content reliably, restoring trust in visual evidence.

Platform algorithms are regulated to limit polarization and amplification of misinformation.

Transparency requirements mandate disclosure of AI use in political campaigns. Voters know when they're being targeted by AI-generated content and can evaluate it accordingly.

AI lowers barriers to democratic participation. Real-time translation, accessible interfaces, and AI assistants that explain complex policy make civic engagement possible for millions previously excluded.

Governments use AI to genuinely understand citizen needs and respond more effectively. Large-scale deliberative processes, facilitated by AI, enable meaningful public input on major decisions.

Democratic institutions have adapted—not by rejecting AI, but by regulating it to serve democratic values. Technology companies face real consequences for amplifying misinformation or enabling manipulation.

Foreign AI-driven interference is detected and countered effectively.

Most importantly, citizens have developed the literacy and critical thinking needed to navigate an AI-mediated information environment. They understand how algorithms work, recognise manipulation tactics, and demand accountability.

Democracy in 2036 doesn't look like democracy in 2024—but it remains genuine. Citizens still govern themselves, informed debate still happens, and power still derives from the consent of the governed.

THE CHOICE WE FACE NOW

Rebecca Adeyemi, watching those election results in Lagos, is living at the inflection point between these two futures.

The technology threatening democracy is the same technology that could strengthen it. AI can manipulate or inform. It can fragment or unify. It can obscure truth or reveal it.

What determines the outcome isn't the technology itself but the choices we make about how it's built, deployed, and governed.

This is the most consequential choice facing humanity in the next decade. Climate change will determine the physical world we inhabit. AI will determine whether we govern ourselves democratically or surrender to algorithmic control we barely understand.

The stakes could not be higher. Democracy is humanity's best—only—mechanism for peaceful self-governance. If it fails, the alternatives are authoritarianism, chaos, or corporate technocracy. None are acceptable.

But democracy's survival is not guaranteed. It requires active defense.

It requires regulation of AI to prevent manipulation. It requires transparency about how algorithmic systems shape information. It requires investment in civic education that prepares citizens for an AI-mediated world. It requires political will to subordinate technological profit to democratic values.

Most fundamentally, it requires citizens who care enough to fight for democratic governance against the considerable forces that would prefer algorithmic control.

The future is not yet determined. Rebecca watching those election results in 2036 could be witnessing democracy's renewal or its funeral.

The technology enabling both futures already exists.

What we choose to do with it in the next few years will determine which future becomes real.

Democracy has survived technological disruption before—printing press, radio, television, internet. It can survive AI. But survival is not automatic. It requires intention, effort, and collective commitment to values that transcend technological efficiency.

The choice ahead is simple to state but difficult to execute: we can use AI to empower citizens or to manipulate them, to expand democracy or to hollow it out, to create informed participation or manufactured consent.

Rebecca's election might be genuinely democratic. But only if we choose, right now, to make it so.

The intelligence age will reshape governance. Whether it strengthens or destroys democracy depends entirely on us.

Chapter 24

WHAT WE MUST DO: CHOICES THAT WILL SHAPE THE NEXT CENTURY

THE WINDOW IS CLOSING

The decisions being made right now—in corporate boardrooms, government agencies, and research Laboratories—will determine how artificial intelligence shapes human society for generations. These decisions are not waiting for public deliberation. They are being made by default, driven by commercial incentives, while most people remain unaware that fundamental choices about their future are being settled without their participation.

This book has documented the extraordinary promise AI offers: healthcare that detects disease earlier, education that adapts to each learner, and systems that might help address climate change. It has also documented the genuine risks: algorithmic discrimination, pervasive surveillance, and job displacement.

Neither the promise nor the peril is inevitable. Both depend on choices.

The real issue is whether those choices will be made deliberately, guided by consideration of human welfare, or made by default through the accumulated momentum of commercial interest. The window for shaping AI's trajectory is narrowing. Once infrastructure is built and dependencies form, changing direction becomes enormously complex.

History offers guidance. From fire to electricity, transformative technologies have moved through similar stages: breakthrough, societal concern, development of expertise, deep integration into civilization, and fundamental transformation of human capability.

WHAT GOVERNMENTS MUST DO

The European Union's AI Act represents one attempt at specificity—requiring risk assessments and human oversight for high-stakes applications. However, regulation must also be adaptive. AI evolves too rapidly for traditional, fixed rules. We need frameworks that can update requirements as capabilities change.

Furthermore, governments must invest in public AI capacity. Regulatory agencies cannot oversee what they do not understand. Currently, technology companies employ thousands of AI specialists while regulatory agencies struggle to hire a handful. This imbalance guarantees that industry will shape governance more than governance shapes industry. Finally, international coordination is essential. AI operates across borders; without global standards, companies will relocate to the least restrictive jurisdictions.

WHAT COMPANIES MUST DO

Transparency must extend beyond marketing materials. Companies should disclose how AI systems work in enough detail that independent researchers can evaluate their behaviour. They should be honest about limitations and acknowledge failures.

Crucially, business models must align with user welfare. When companies profit from data collection irrespective of privacy, surveillance becomes a business strategy. Different models—subscription services, usage fees, or public utility frameworks—can better align corporate interests with the public good.

WHAT INDIVIDUALS MUST DO

Individual actions aggregate into market signals. What people demand, and what they refuse to accept, determines which corporate strategies succeed.

Understanding AI's basic workings matters. Most people do not need to understand neural network architectures, but they must recognise that AI systems learn from data and reproduce patterns in that data. Critical consumption of AI-generated content is now essential. As synthetic media becomes indistinguishable from reality, reflexive trust is dangerous.

Seeking primary sources and questioning dramatic claims are habits that matter more than ever.

Political engagement also shapes governance. Voting for candidates who understand technology's implications and contacting MPs about AI-related legislation are the only ways to ensure that governments regulate effectively rather than deferring to industry preferences.

EDUCATION FOR AN AI WORLD

Educational systems designed for the industrial era cannot prepare people for an AI-transformed economy. The skills that served previous generations—memorising information and performing routine cognitive tasks—are precisely those that AI systems now handle.

Education must shift towards capabilities that remain distinctively human:
- Critical Thinking: The ability to evaluate sources, identify biases, and form independent judgements.

- Creativity: Identifying problems worth solving and making creative leaps that combine different domains in unexpected ways.

- Emotional Intelligence: Understanding human motivation, building trust, and providing emotional support.

Continuous learning must become the norm. When the skills that matter keep changing, education cannot be a one-time investment completed in youth. Accessible, affordable opportunities for ongoing development are now essential infrastructure.

DISTRIBUTING BENEFITS BROADLY

The central political question of the AI era is how the value generated by AI gets distributed. Left to market forces, the gains will concentrate among those who own the systems.

David Parker's perspective on "what we must do" is shaped by lived experience, not abstract policy debates. He knows what it feels like when the social safety net catches you—barely—and what it feels like when it doesn't.

"We need transition support that's actually adequate," he says when asked. "Not six months of retraining while your savings evaporate. Not programmes that assume everyone can afford to live on reduced income while learning new skills. We need systems that recognise: if you spent twenty years building expertise that AI eliminated, society owes you more than a government website with job listings."

He's become an advocate, somewhat to his surprise, speaking at community meetings about AI's workforce impact. His message is practical: stronger unemployment insurance, portable benefits, guaranteed income during retraining, and actual job placement assistance rather than empty promises.

"The companies deploying these systems are profiting immensely," David points out. "Those profits should fund support for the workers they're displacing. Not out of charity—out of basic fairness. If AI creates enormous wealth, that wealth should support the people whose jobs financed its development."

He's not anti-technology. He's pro-human dignity. And he's living proof that without deliberate policy choices, AI's benefits will flow upward while its costs flow downward, creating a society more divided, more precarious, and more unjust than the one we're leaving behind.

Progressive taxation of AI-generated profits represents one mechanism for distribution. Companies that achieve massive productivity gains through AI generate wealth that society helped create through public investment in basic research. Taxing a portion of that wealth to fund public goods—healthcare, education, and safety nets—distributes benefits beyond shareholders. Proposals like Universal Basic Income (UBI) must be seriously debated as a response to a world where Labour markets may no longer be able to absorb everyone.

PRESERVING HUMAN AGENCY

Human oversight provides one safeguard. We must insist that humans remain "in the loop" for consequential decisions. But oversight must be meaningful; "rubber-stamping" an AI decision we don't understand is no check at all. We must also deliberately maintain zones of life free from AI optimisation—spaces where human relationships and spontaneity flourish without algorithmic mediation. Technology should serve human values, not the other way around.

THE STAKES

History offers grounds for optimism. Previous technological revolutions eventually spread benefits more broadly—but only because people organised and demanded it. Labour movements fought for rights; governments regulated monopolies. Benefits did not distribute themselves.

The same will be true for AI. The technology doesn't determine the outcome. Human choices do. We must make those choices consciously and collectively—before the window closes.

Chapter 25

THE FUTURE WE CHOOSE:
TWO PATHS AHEAD

MORNING IN TWO WORLDS

Consider two possible futures for Maya Chen, both set in 2036 when she is still twelve years old. In one world, Maya wakes to an AI assistant that has learned her patterns over the years. It knows she has a maths test today and that she learns best with a morning review. It presents practice problems tailored to her learning style and encourages her without pressure. Her mother, working from home as a designer, uses AI tools that have tripled her productivity— she earns more while working fewer hours than her own mother did. Maya's grandmother lives independently in her own home, supported by monitoring systems that caught a heart irregularity three months ago, preventing a stroke. The family is closer because AI handles the logistics and bureaucracy, leaving more time for the human connection that matters.

In another world, Maya wakes to an AI assistant that knows her patterns too—but this knowledge serves different purposes. The system optimises for engagement metrics that generate advertising revenue. It shows her content calculated to hold her attention regardless of its educational value. Her mother works longer hours than ever because her company's AI has intensified productivity expectations rather than sharing gains with workers. Maya's grandmother was forced into a care home two years ago because her family couldn't afford the AI monitoring systems that enable independent living. The family sees each other less because AI has made work more demanding, while the benefits flow elsewhere.

Same technology. Different outcomes. The difference lies in the choices made between now and then.

THE OPTIMISTIC PATH

In this future, healthcare reaches everyone earlier. AI systems detect diseases before symptoms appear, and diagnostic capabilities once reserved for specialists are available in rural clinics. Education adapts to each learner rather than forcing all students through the same curriculum at the same pace. Adults retrain for new careers throughout their lives, supported by AI tutors that make expertise accessible to anyone.

Work becomes more humane as AI handles routine tasks while humans focus on creativity, connection, and judgement. Productivity gains translate into shorter work weeks rather than intensified demands. Environmental challenges become manageable as smart grids integrate renewable energy seamlessly and transportation systems move people with minimal emissions. Communities become stronger as geographic barriers to connection dissolve and the loneliness epidemic gives way to new forms of support.

THE PESSIMISTIC PATH

In this future, AI healthcare exists but serves only those who can pay.

Education becomes a surveillance system that sorts children into tracks from an early age, using AI assessments that encode historical biases.

The promise of personalised learning becomes the reality of personalised tracking.

Work intensifies as algorithmic management optimises for efficiency without regard for human well-being. A growing population finds itself economically unnecessary, watching wealth concentrate among the few.

Environmental promises prove hollow as AI's energy demands offset efficiency gains elsewhere. Privacy effectively ends as surveillance becomes total. Every movement becomes data harvested for commercial exploitation, and something essential about human freedom quietly dies.

THE REALISTIC PATH

Some applications will work well. AI medical diagnosis will save lives; AI tutoring will help students who would otherwise struggle. Other applications will cause harm despite good intentions. Algorithmic systems will discriminate in ways their creators didn't anticipate.

Efficiency gains will concentrate among those with the power to capture them.

The mixed reality is not a reason for complacency; it is a description of the terrain where choices matter. Aggregate outcomes depend on countless individual decisions, but those decisions are shaped by the policies and social expectations that collective action can influence.

Every major technology has traced a similar path: the moment of

breakthrough, the period of uncertainty and resistance, the gradual accumulation of expertise and best practices, the point where reversal becomes unthinkable, and finally the reshaping of what it means to be human.

The Industrial Revolution initially devastated skilled craftsmen and created unprecedented inequality. But over the decades, Labour movements won protections, and productivity gains eventually raised living standards. Electricity initially served only the wealthy, but regulation made it a public utility that benefited everyone. The internet began as a promise of democratised connection but became a complex landscape of harvested data and platform power.

AI is earlier in this cycle. The initial disruption is underway. The concentration of benefits is visible. The social and political response is just beginning. How this story ends depends on whether we learn from history or merely repeat it.

Sarah Chen attended her first city council meeting on AI governance feeling both hopeful and apprehensive. As an urban planner, she'd watched algorithms reshape her field—mostly for good, but with concerning blind spots around equity and community input.

"These systems are making decisions about our neighbourhoods," she told the council. "Where to route transit, where to concentrate police presence, which permits to fast-track. But who programmed the priorities? Who decided what 'optimal' means? And who's accountable when the algorithm's recommendation serves some communities while neglecting others?"

The council members nodded, but Sarah could see their glazed uncertainty. They understood democracy; they didn't understand neural networks. The gap between governing intelligence and comprehending intelligence was growing wider, and Sarah wasn't sure how to bridge it.

She thinks about Maya, now twelve and growing up with AI as infrastructure rather than innovation. Maya's generation will inherit decisions being made now about transparency, accountability, and control. Sarah wants those decisions made democratically, with real public input, not just technical experts optimising for abstract metrics.

But democracy requires informed citizens, and Sarah herself barely grasps how the systems reshaping her city actually work. She can see their effects, question their priorities, advocate for alternatives—but she can't audit their logic or verify their fairness. That dependency troubles her more than any specific AI system.

When intelligence becomes too complex to understand, how do citizens govern it?

THE CHOICE IS YOURS

This book has tried to show you what AI is—neither the marketing hype nor the science fiction fears, but the complex reality of a technology that will transform virtually every aspect of human life.

You have seen the history that brought us to this moment—fire, the wheel, metal, steam, electricity, and computers—each extending human capability. AI continues this progression, extending cognitive capability as previous technologies extended physical capability. You have seen applications in healthcare, education, work, and cities. You have seen that the technology doesn't determine outcomes—human choices do.

Now you face your own decisions. How you engage with AI affects your own life. How you participate in democratic processes shapes the governance that constrains or enables different futures. How you think about what matters— meaning, connection, and freedom—determines what you will accept and what you will demand.

The future is not fixed. It remains open to human agency and deliberate choice. The next decade will shape possibilities for the rest of the century.

Fire gave humanity power over nature. The wheel gave mobility. Metal gave tools. Steam gave industrial might. Electricity gave light.

Computers gave information. Now, AI offers extended intelligence. What we do with this gift will define the century ahead. We can use it to reduce suffering and expand opportunity, or we can allow it to undermine the freedom that enables human flourishing.

The Age of Intelligence has begun. The future it creates is the one we choose.

LETTER FROM 2036

1 5th December 2036 Edinburgh, Scotland Dear Reader from 2026, You probably want to know how it all turned out. I would have wanted to know back when I was reading predictions about the AI revolution supposedly coming. So let me tell you what I can see from here—ten years into the transformation that was beginning when you started reading this book.

My name is Laura Ashby. I'm a climate scientist—or I was, before the categories blurred. Now I am something more challenging to define: a person who works with AI systems to understand Earth's climate, interpret what the models reveal, and translate that understanding into guidance that policymakers can use. My job didn't exist ten years ago.

Neither did most of what I do every day.

The first thing I want to say is that the predictions were both right and wrong. AI transformed everything, as the optimists promised. It also created problems that the enthusiasts dismissed, as the sceptics warned.

What no one captured was how ordinary it would all feel by the time we arrived. The extraordinary became mundane so gradually that I sometimes forget how different life was before.

I wake up in the morning, and my home has already adjusted the temperature based on my sleep patterns. My AI assistant has sorted my messages and drafted responses to routine requests that I can review with a single tap. I don't think about any of this. It just happens, the way electricity occurs when you flip a switch.

My mother is eighty-two years old and lives alone in the house where I grew up. I worried constantly about her ten years ago—whether she'd fall or whether she was lonely. Now her home monitors her health so unobtrusively that she forgets the systems exist. When her heart rhythm showed an irregularity three years ago, her AI caught it before she noticed symptoms. The early intervention probably added years to her life. She is more connected to her family now than she was when she was younger.

My daughter is fifteen. She's learning in ways I never could have imagined—AI tutors that adapt to exactly how her mind works, letting her race ahead in subjects where she's ready and slow down where she needs more time. The gap between what she takes for granted and what amazed me at her age is enormous.

My brother lost his job in 2028. He'd been a financial analyst—good at his work and providing well for his family. Then AI systems became good enough that his firm no longer needed as many analysts. He wasn't replaced exactly; his role just gradually shrank until it disappeared.

The transition was brutal. He spent two years struggling to find comparable work, watching his confidence erode. He eventually found a new path—he now helps small businesses navigate AI tools. He's okay now. But those two years were among the hardest of his life.

The inequality you're already seeing has worsened in some ways and improved in others. AI in healthcare is remarkable, but access still depends on what you can afford. Premium AI systems serve the wealthy; everyone else gets what is available through the NHS or basic commercial offerings. The technology exists to give everyone excellent care. The will to make that happen remains contested.

Privacy is different now. I've mostly accepted that my digital life is comprehensively tracked. I made trade-offs—convenience and capability in exchange for information about my patterns. We talk less about privacy now, not because we stopped caring, but because fighting felt futile. I'm not sure we were right about that. Some days, I miss the version of privacy that once existed.

The truth is more complicated to find than it once was. Synthetic media is so good now that video evidence means almost nothing. I've learned to be sceptical of everything I see online. The baseline assumption that you could believe your own eyes is gone.

My work gives me a particular perspective on AI's impact on the climate.

AI helps us optimise energy grids and design efficient buildings. It's contributed to measurable improvements. But AI itself consumes vast amounts of energy and water. The data centres that power this transformation have a significant environmental footprint. I can't tell you AI has solved the climate crisis. I can only tell you it's given us better tools for a fight that remains undecided.

Here's what I wish I could have told myself ten years ago: the transformation was fundamental, but life still feels like life. The problems didn't disappear; they changed form. The technology amplified what was already present—good and evil, fair and unfair. What mattered most wasn't the technology itself. It was the choices people made about how to use it.

If I could send you one message from 2036, it would be this: The future isn't predetermined. You are living through the period when the patterns will be set. What you demand, what you accept, and what you refuse to tolerate— these will shape what's possible for my daughter and her children.

The technology doesn't decide. You do.

The Age of Intelligence arrived. What we did with it became who we are.

Make it count.

Laura Ashby Edinburgh, 2036

LET'S CONTINUE THE CONVERSATION

Thank you for joining me on this journey from the ancient hearths of our ancestors to the intelligent landscapes of 2036.

As I wrote in the preceding chapters, the future of artificial intelligence is not a destination we are merely travelling towards—it is a world we are creating through our collective decisions. I would love to hear your thoughts on what that world should look like.

Whether you have a question about a specific chapter, a reflection on your own vision for the next decade, or want to share how AI is currently touching your life or profession, please do get in touch.

Contact Gerard: Email: reader@theageofintelligence.ie Please note: While the volume of correspondence and my speaking schedule mean I may not be able to provide a personal response to every email, please know that I read every message and value the perspectives shared by my readers.

A Small Favour: If this book sparked a new idea or helped you see the future differently, please consider leaving a review on Amazon or Goodreads. For independent authors, your words are the most powerful way to help other readers discover this work.

I look forward to hearing from you.

— Gerard McNamara

Website: theageofintelligence.ie | Email: reader@theageofintelligence.ie

Coming Next: The Age of Transition

The Age of Intelligence asked who owns AI. The next book asks what it does to us — our work, our identity, and our sense of purpose. The Age of Transition: Work, Identity, and the Human Cost of a World Remade by AI is forthcoming. For updates and early access, visit theageofintelligence.ie/next-book

Throughout this book, I've described how artificial intelligence will transform nearly every aspect of life. That transformation is already underway. The question isn't whether to engage with it—you already are, whether you realise it or not. The question is whether you'll engage thoughtfully or be swept along by changes you don't understand.

This appendix offers practical steps you can take today. Not predictions about the future, but concrete actions. Some take minutes; others require sustained effort over months or years. All of them will help you navigate the intelligence age more effectively.

UNDERSTAND THE TECHNOLOGY

You don't need to become a computer scientist, but basic AI literacy is becoming as important as basic financial literacy. Here's where to start: Use AI tools yourself. The best way to understand AI's capabilities and limitations is direct experience. Try ChatGPT, Claude, or similar assistants. Ask them to help with real tasks: drafting emails, explaining complex topics, brainstorming ideas. Notice what they do well and where they fail. This hands-on experience is worth more than any amount of reading about AI.

Learn to spot AI-generated content. As AI-generated text, images, and videos become ubiquitous, the ability to identify them becomes crucial.

Look for telltale signs: text that's fluent but vague, images with subtle anatomical errors, videos where lighting doesn't quite match.

Practice this skill now, while the technology is still imperfect enough to leave traces.

Follow developments critically. AI is evolving rapidly, and much of what you read about it is either hype or fear-mongering. Develop sources you trust. I recommend starting with researchers who explain their work clearly: Melanie Mitchell, Gary Marcus, and Fei-Fei Li offer balanced perspectives. Be sceptical of both breathless enthusiasm and apocalyptic warnings.

PROTECT YOURSELF

AI creates new vulnerabilities alongside its benefits. Basic digital hygiene matters more than ever: Strengthen your defences against AI-powered scams. Voice cloning and deepfakes make impersonation trivially easy. Establish verification protocols with family members—a code word or question only you would know. Be suspicious of urgent requests, even if the voice sounds exactly like someone you trust. When in doubt, hang up and call back using a number you know is genuine.

Audit your digital footprint. AI systems learn from data, and much of that data comes from you. Review your privacy settings on social media.

Consider what you share and with whom. Remember that anything you post may train future AI systems. You can't take back what's already public, but you can be more thoughtful going forward.

Understand how AI systems make decisions about you. Credit scores, insurance rates, job applications, and medical diagnoses increasingly involve AI. You have the right to know when AI is being used in decisions that affect you. Ask. If the answer is unclear, push for clarity. In many jurisdictions, you have legal rights to explanation and appeal.

DEVELOP DURABLE SKILLS

Some skills will remain valuable regardless of how AI develops. Invest in these: Cultivate judgement. AI can process information and generate options, but deciding what matters requires human judgement. Practice making decisions with incomplete information. Develop your ability to weigh competing values and priorities. Learn to recognise when a problem requires creativity versus when it requires discipline.

Strengthen interpersonal abilities. Empathy, negotiation, leadership, and the ability to build trust—these remain distinctly human. AI can simulate warmth, but it cannot genuinely care. In an increasingly automated world, the ability to connect authentically with other humans becomes more valuable, not less.

Learn to work with AI, not against it. The most effective professionals won't be those who resist AI or those who defer to it entirely, but those who learn to colLabourate with it effectively. This means understanding what AI does well (pattern recognition, information synthesis, rapid iteration) and what humans do better (setting goals, understanding context, making ethical judgements).

Stay adaptable. The specific skills that matter will shift as AI capabilities evolve. What won't change is the need to keep learning.

Cultivate curiosity. Build the habit of acquiring new skills throughout your life. The most important ability may be the meta-skill of learning itself.

PREPARE YOUR CAREER

AI will transform every profession. Here's how to position yourself: Honestly assess your exposure. Which parts of your job involve routine information processing? Those are most vulnerable to automation. Which parts require judgement, creativity, or human connection? Those are more durable. Don't assume your profession is safe because it requires education or expertise—AI is particularly good at tasks that educated professionals do.

Build a portfolio of capabilities. Don't bet your career on a single skill. Develop complementary abilities that together create unique value. A lawyer who understands technology, can communicate clearly, and builds strong client relationships is far more secure than one who only knows the law.

Consider adjacent opportunities. As AI transforms industries, new roles emerge at the boundaries. Someone who understands both healthcare and AI can help hospitals implement new systems. Someone who grasps both education and technology can design better learning experiences. Look for intersections where your existing knowledge meets emerging needs.

Have a backup plan. Even with preparation, disruption may come faster than expected. Maintain financial reserves. Keep your network active.

Stay informed about opportunities in other fields. Hope for the best, but prepare for significant change.

ENGAGE AS A CITIZEN

The choices society makes about AI will affect everyone. Your voice matters: Educate yourself on AI policy. Understand the debates: Should AI systems require human oversight? How should we handle AI-generated misinformation? What rights do workers have as jobs transform? You don't need to become an expert, but you should understand the basic trade-offs.

Support thoughtful regulation. AI development is currently governed primarily by the companies building it. That's not sustainable. Advocate for regulatory frameworks that ensure safety without stifling innovation. Support politicians who take AI seriously but aren't captured by either tech industry interests or reflexive technophobia.

Participate in your democracy. Vote. Contact your representatives about AI issues. Join organisations working on AI governance. The decisions being made now will shape the technology for decades. If you don't participate, others will make those decisions for you.

Demand transparency. When AI systems affect you—in hiring, lending, healthcare, or justice—you deserve to understand how. Push for explainable AI. Support requirements that companies disclose when AI is making significant decisions. Transparency won't solve every problem, but secrecy makes accountability impossible.

PRESERVE WHAT MATTERS

Finally, remember that not everything should be optimised:

Protect spaces for human connection. Not every conversation needs to be efficient. Not every relationship needs to be mediated by technology.

Maintain friendships that exist in person, activities that don't involve screens, conversations that meander without purpose. These are not inefficiencies to be eliminated; they are what make life meaningful.

Cultivate attention. AI systems are designed to capture and hold your attention—it's how they generate value for their creators. Protect your ability to focus. Practice doing one thing at a time. Read books.

Have conversations without checking your phone. Your attention is finite and precious; don't surrender it thoughtlessly.

Stay grounded in physical reality. Walk outside. Work with your hands.

Notice the weather, the seasons, the way light changes through the day.

As more of life moves into digital spaces, maintaining connection to the physical world becomes an act of resistance—and a source of wellbeing that no virtual environment can replicate.

Remember what matters. AI can help you live more efficiently, but it cannot tell you what to live for. That's your job. Take time to clarify your values. What kind of person do you want to be? What relationships do you want to nurture? What would make your life meaningful? No algorithm can answer these questions for you.

–The intelligence age is not something that will happen to you. It's something you're already living through. The actions you take—starting today—will determine whether AI enhances your life or diminishes it, whether it expands your capabilities or erodes your agency.

You have more power than you might think. Use it wisely.

SOURCES AND FURTHER READING

GENERAL WORKS ON ARTIFICIAL INTELLIGENCE - BOSTROM, NICK. SUPERINTELLIGENCE: PATHS, DANGERS, STRATEGIES.

Oxford University Press, 2014. (The foundational text on long-term AI risks) - Mitchell, Melanie. Artificial Intelligence: A Guide for Thinking Humans. Pelican, 2019. (An accessible introduction to AI limitations) - Russell, Stuart. Human Compatible: Artificial Intelligence and the Problem of Control. Viking, 2019. (Essential reading on AI alignment) - Tegmark, Max. Life 3.0: Being Human in the Age of Artificial Intelligence. Allen Lane, 2017.

Part One: The Foundations of Progress (Chapters 2–6) - Allen, Robert C. The British Industrial Revolution in Global Perspective. Cambridge University Press, 2009.

• Bulliet, Richard W. The Wheel: Inventions and Reinventions. Columbia University Press, 2016.

• Isaacson, Walter. The Innovators: How a Group of Hackers, Geniuses and Geeks Created the Digital Revolution. Simon & Schuster, 2014.

• Nye, David E. Electrifying America: Social Meanings of a New Technology. MIT Press, 1990.

• Robb, John. The Early Mediterranean Village. Cambridge University Press, 2007. (Neolithic metallurgy and craft specialisation) - Turing, Alan. "Computing Machinery and Intelligence." Mind, vol. 59, no. 236, 1950, pp. 433–460.

• Wrangham, Richard. Catching Fire: How Cooking Made Us Human. Profile Books, 2009.

Part Two: AI in Daily Life (Chapters 7–9) - Stilgoe, Jack. Who's Driving Innovation? New Technologies and the Collaborative State. Palgrave Macmillan, 2020. (Autonomous vehicle regulation) - Turkle, Sherry. Alone Together: Why We Expect More from Technology and Less from Each Other. Basic Books, 2011.

• Statistics on smart home adoption and autonomous vehicles are sourced from the International Energy Agency (IEA) and the McKinsey Global Institute.

Part Three: AI in Society (Chapters 10–15) - Autor, David H. "Why Are There Still So Many Jobs? The History and Future of Workplace Automation." Journal of Economic Perspectives, vol. 29, no. 3, 2015, pp. 3–30.

• Frey, Carl Benedikt, and Michael A. Osborne. "The Future of Employment: How Susceptible Are Jobs to Computerization?" Technological Forecasting and Social Change, vol. 114, 2017, pp. 254–280.

• Holmes, Wayne, et al. Artificial Intelligence in Education: Promises and Implications for Teaching and Learning. Centre for Curriculum Redesign, 2019.

• Obermeyer, Ziad, et al. "Dissecting Racial Bias in an Algorithm Used to Manage the Health of Populations." Science, vol. 366, no. 6464, 2019, pp. 447–453.

• Sixsmith, Andrew, and Judith Sixsmith. "Aging in Place in the United Kingdom." Aging International, vol. 33, 2008, pp. 219–235.

• Topol, Eric. Deep Medicine: How Artificial Intelligence Can Make Healthcare Human Again. Basic Books, 2019.

> **Chapter 11: AI and Mental Health** - Sources and Further Reading ###
AI Therapy Clinical Trials:
• Heinz, M., & Jacobson, N. "First-ever clinical trial of generative AI-powered therapy chatbot."NEJM AI, March 27, 2025. NEJM AI Research Study
• Dartmouth Research News. "First therapy chatbot trial yields mental health benefits."Dartmouth: Therapy Chatbot Trial ### Social Media and Mental Health Impact:

• U.S. Surgeon General's Advisory. "Social Media and Youth Mental Health."2023. U.S. Surgeon General: Youth Mental Health & Social Media

• The Wall Street Journal. "Facebook Files: Instagram toxic for teen girls."September 2021. The Verge: Facebook/Instagram Teen Mental Health Research

• Center for Countering Digital Hate. "TikTok algorithm study: Self-harm content."2022. https://www.theguardian.com/technology/2022/dec/15/tiktok-self-harm-study-results-every-parents-nightmare

• Amnesty International. "TikTok steering children towards depressive and suicidal content."2025. Amnesty International: TikTok and Children's Mental Health ### AI Usage for Mental Health Support:

• Sentio University. "Survey: ChatGPT the largest provider of mental health support in the United States."February 2025. Sentio University AI Research Survey

• RAND Corporation. "One in Eight Adolescents and Young Adults Use AI Chatbots for Mental Health Advice."2025. RAND Corporation: Adolescents and AI Chatbots ### Global Mental Health Crisis:

• World Health Organization. "Over a billion people living with mental health conditions."2025. World Health Organization: Mental Health Conditions

• WHO Global Health Observatory. "Mental health workers - Data by country."https://apps.who.int/gho/data/view.main. HWF11v ### Historical and Technological Context:

• Obschonka, M., & Stuetzer, M. "Industrial Revolution's psychological impact."Journal of Personality and Social Psychology, 2017. Cambridge: Industrial Revolution Psychological Impact

• Nature Scientific Data. "Digital phenotyping data for mental health monitoring."2025. Nature: Research Article > Chapter 23: AI and Democracy - Sources and Further Reading ### Election Interference and Deepfakes:

• Associated Press. "AI-generated robocalls mimicking Biden's voice disrupt New Hampshire primary."January 2024. AP News: New Hampshire AI Robocalls

• BBC. "Deepfake video of Zelensky telling Ukrainians to surrender debunked."March 2022. BBC: Technology Report

• Deutsche Welle. "Fact check: Turkey's Erdogan shows false Kilicdaroglu video."May 2023. https://www.dw.com/en/fact-check-turkeys-erdogan-shows-false-kilicdaroglu-video/a-65554034

• The Conversation. "Deepfakes and disinformation swirl ahead of Indonesian election."2024. The Conversation: Deepfakes and Disinformation
• WIRED. "Indian Voters Are Being Bombarded With Millions of Deepfakes."2024. Wired: Indian Elections AI Deepfakes ### AI and Democratic Threats:
• Berkeley Funginstitute. "Social media algorithms and their effects on American politics."Berkeley Fung Institute: Social Media Algorithms ### AI for Democratic Enhancement:
• New America. "Civic Assemblies in Action: Lessons on Civic Engagement from Fort Collins."2025. New America: Civic Assemblies
• Microsoft Case Study. "Government of the City of Buenos Aires - Azure OpenAI Service."2025. https://www.microsoft.com/en/customers/story/21596-government-of-the-city-of-buenos-aires-azure-open-ai-service
• OECD Observatory of Public Sector Innovation. "Boti - The City's WhatsApp."OECD: Boti WhatsApp Innovation ### AI Lobbying and Regulation:
• OpenSecrets.org. "OpenAI Lobbying Summary."2026. OpenSecrets: Federal Lobbying Data
• MIT Technology Review. "OpenAI ups its lobbying efforts nearly seven-fold."January 2025. https://www.technologyreview.com/2025/01/21/1110260/openai-ups-its-lobbying-efforts-nearly-seven-fold/

Part Four: AI in the World (Chapters 16–20) - International Energy Agency. "Electricity 2024: Analysis and Forecast to 2026." IEA, 2024. (Projections for data centre power consumption) - Li, Pengfei, et al. "Making AI Less Thirsty: Uncovering and Addressing the Secret Water Footprint of AI Models." arXiv preprint, 2023.
• Municipal statistics for Singapore, Amsterdam, London, and Barcelona are sourced from municipal government evaluations (2020–2024).

Part Five: The Choice Ahead (Chapters 21–25) - Angwin, Julia, et al. "Machine Bias." ProPublica, 23 May 2016. (The COMPAS investigation).

• Buolamwini, Joy, and Timnit Gebru. "Gender Shades: Intersectional Accuracy Disparities in Commercial Gender Classification." Proceedings of Machine Learning Research, vol. 81, 2018, pp. 1–15.

• Dastin, Jeffrey. "Amazon Scraps Secret AI Recruiting Tool That Showed Bias Against Women." Reuters, 10 October 2018.
• European Union. "Regulation (EU) 2024/1689 Laying Down Harmonised Rules on Artificial Intelligence (AI Act)." Official Journal of the European Union, 2024.
• Hill, Kashmir. "Wrongfully Accused by an Algorithm." The New York Times, 24 June 2020.
• Zuboff, Shoshana. The Age of Surveillance Capitalism. Profile Books, 2019.

FURTHER READING & RESEARCH INSTITUTES - THE AI NOW INSTITUTE (AINOWINSTITUTE. ORG) - THE CENTRE FOR THE GOVERNANCE OF AI, OXFORD UNIVERSITY (GOVERNANCE. AI)

GLOSSARY

The following terms appear throughout this book. These definitions are intended to be accessible rather than technically exhaustive.

Algorithm: A set of step-by-step instructions that a computer follows to solve a problem or complete a task. Traditional algorithms are explicitly programmed by humans; machine learning algorithms learn from data.

Alignment: The challenge of ensuring AI systems pursue goals that match human values and intentions. A misaligned AI might achieve its programmed objective in ways that harm humans or violate our values.

Artificial General Intelligence (AGI): A hypothetical AI system capable of performing any intellectual task a human can do. Unlike current 'narrow' AI systems that excel at specific tasks, AGI would possess broad, flexible intelligence. AGI does not yet exist.

Artificial Intelligence (AI): Computer systems designed to perform tasks that typically require human intelligence, such as understanding language, recognising images, making decisions, or learning from experience.

Autonomous System: A machine or software that can operate and make decisions without continuous human control. Examples range from self-driving cars to AI systems that manage financial trades.

Bias (in AI): Systematic errors in AI systems that produce unfair outcomes, often reflecting prejudices present in training data or the assumptions of system designers. AI bias can discriminate based on race, gender, age, or other characteristics.

Big Data: Datasets too large or complex for traditional data-processing methods. The availability of big data has been crucial to recent AI advances, as machine learning systems require vast amounts of information to identify patterns.

Black Box: An AI system whose internal decision-making process cannot be easily understood or explained. Many modern AI systems, particularly deep learning models, operate as black boxes, making it difficult to know why they reach specific conclusions.

Chatbot: An AI program designed to simulate conversation with humans, typically through text. Modern chatbots powered by large language models can engage in sophisticated dialogue on a wide range of topics.

Cloud Computing: Delivering computing services—including storage, processing power, and software—over the internet. Cloud computing enables AI systems to access vast computational resources on demand.

Computer Vision: AI systems that can interpret and understand visual information from the world, such as photographs, videos, or real-time camera feeds. Applications include facial recognition, medical image analysis, and autonomous vehicles.

Data Centre: A facility housing computer systems and associated components, including servers, storage systems, and networking equipment. Large-scale AI requires enormous data centres that consume significant electricity and water.

Deep Learning: A subset of machine learning using artificial neural networks with many layers (hence 'deep'). Deep learning has driven most recent AI breakthroughs, from image recognition to language understanding.

Deepfake: AI-generated synthetic media—typically video or audio—that convincingly depicts someone saying or doing something they never actually said or did. Named for the 'deep learning' techniques used to create them.

Deployment: The process of making an AI system available for real-world use after development and testing. Deployment decisions determine who can access AI capabilities and under what conditions.

Emergent Behaviour: Capabilities that appear in AI systems without being explicitly programmed, often arising unexpectedly as models grow larger. Some researchers view emergence as evidence of AI progress; others question whether it represents genuine new capabilities.

Explainable AI (XAI): AI systems designed to provide understandable explanations for their decisions. Explainability is crucial in high-stakes domains like healthcare and criminal justice, where people need to understand why AI reached particular conclusions.

Generative AI: AI systems that create new content—text, images, music, video, or code—rather than simply analysing existing data.

Large language models and image generators are prominent examples.

Hallucination: When an AI system generates plausible-sounding but false or nonsensical information. Large language models are particularly prone to hallucination, confidently stating 'facts' that are entirely fabricated.

High-Frequency Trading (HFT): Automated trading systems that execute large numbers of orders at extremely high speeds, often holding positions for only fractions of a second. HFT relies on algorithms to identify and exploit tiny market inefficiencies.

Large Language Model (LLM): An AI system trained on vast amounts of text to understand and generate human language. Examples include GPT-4, Claude, and Gemini. LLMs power modern chatbots and many text-generation applications.

Machine Learning: A subset of AI where systems learn from data rather than being explicitly programmed. Instead of following predetermined rules, machine learning algorithms identify patterns in examples and apply those patterns to new situations.

Model: In AI, a mathematical representation that has been trained to perform a specific task. A 'language model' has learned patterns in text; an 'image model' has learned patterns in pictures.

Moore's Law: The observation that the number of transistors on computer chips roughly doubles every two years, leading to exponential increases in computing power. While not a physical law, this trend held for decades and drove much of the digital revolution.

Natural Language Processing (NLP): AI techniques for understanding, interpreting, and generating human language. NLP enables applications like machine translation, sentiment analysis, and conversational AI.

Neural Network: A computing system loosely inspired by biological brains, consisting of interconnected nodes ('neurons') that process information. Neural networks learn by adjusting the strength of connections between nodes based on training data.

Optimisation: The process of finding the best solution from a set of possibilities. AI systems often work by optimising for specified objectives—which is why defining those objectives correctly is crucial.

Parameter: A variable in an AI model that is learned during training. Modern large language models have hundreds of billions of parameters, each representing a small piece of learned knowledge or pattern.

Pattern Recognition: The ability to identify regularities in data.

Much of what AI does well involves recognising patterns that humans might miss due to the volume or complexity of information.

Prompt: The input or instruction given to a generative AI system.

'Prompt engineering' refers to the skill of crafting inputs that produce desired outputs from AI systems.

Reinforcement Learning: A machine learning approach where systems learn by receiving rewards or penalties for their actions, similar to how animals learn through trial and error. Used to train game-playing AI and robotic systems.

Reshoring: The practice of returning manufacturing to a company's home country after it had been moved abroad. AI-driven automation is accelerating reshoring by reducing the importance of Labour costs.

Singularity: A hypothetical future point when AI becomes capable of recursive self-improvement, potentially leading to rapid, uncontrollable technological change. The concept remains highly speculative and contested.

Superintelligence: A hypothetical AI system that vastly exceeds human intelligence across all domains. Whether superintelligence is possible, and what it might mean for humanity, is a subject of intense debate.

Surveillance Capitalism: An economic system where personal data is extracted and used to predict and influence behaviour for profit. Term coined by Shoshana Zuboff to describe the business model of major technology companies.

Training: The process by which AI systems learn from data. During training, a model adjusts its parameters to better perform its intended task. Training modern AI systems requires enormous computational resources.

Training Data: The information used to teach an AI system. The quality, quantity, and characteristics of training data profoundly affect what the resulting AI can do and how it behaves.

Transformer: A neural network architecture introduced in 2017 that revolutionised natural language processing. Transformers enable models to process entire sequences of text simultaneously, making them far more capable than previous approaches. GPT stands for 'Generative Pre-trained Transformer.' Turing Test: A test of machine intelligence proposed by Alan Turing in 1950. A machine passes if a human evaluator cannot reliably distinguish its responses from those of a human. While influential historically, the test is now considered an inadequate measure of AI capability.

ABOUT THE AUTHOR

Gerard McNamara has spent over thirty years in the high-volume electronics industry, where he built a career at the intersection of technology and business management. His work gave him a front-row seat to the cycles of transformation that define the sector — and a practitioner's understanding of how quickly the unimaginable becomes the everyday.

He has been involved in computer hardware for more than a decade, and his interest in computing stretches back considerably further. He watched the industry evolve from the command-line days of DOS through the early graphical interfaces of Windows 3.1, through the internet revolution, and into today's era of machine learning and generative AI — capabilities that would have seemed like science fiction just ten years ago.

That long perspective is what shaped this book. Having witnessed several waves of technological change from the inside, McNamara recognised that the current AI transformation was following a pattern he had seen before — but at a speed and scale that demanded a different kind of attention. Not the breathless enthusiasm of Silicon Valley futurism, and not the paralysing anxiety of worst-case speculation, but a clear-eyed look at who was building the systems, who would own them, and what that would mean for the rest of us.

The Age of Intelligence is the result: a book written not from the academy or the start-up pitch deck, but from decades of watching how technology actually embeds itself into industries, institutions, and daily life — and what happens when society recognises the dependency too late.

McNamara lives in Ireland. This is his first book.

Contact: reader@theageofintelligence.ie

Website: www.theageofintelligence.ie

9 781919 524511